JEET KUNE DO
PURE & SIMPLE

JASON KOROL

CORNERSTONE
JEET KUNE DO

JEET KUNE DO: PURE & SIMPLE

Cover design, book design, and original fantastic artwork by Devin Smith
www.artofdevin.com

Photography by James Schoeni*
*Excluding images on pages 29 and 31

Editing by Christy Strickland

For information, visit www.cornerstonejkd.com.

INTRODUCTION

There's a story about Sherlock Holmes and Watson that I think we should consider before we get started on our inquiry of Bruce Lee's Jeet Kune Do.

One night Holmes and Watson went camping, enjoyed some food and refreshments and then went to sleep. In the middle of the night Holmes woke up and noticed the multitude of stars above his head. Seeing this he jabbed an elbow into his cohort's side. "Watson, Watson," he said, "what do you see?"

"Endless stars," replied Watson.

"And what does that tell you?"

"Well, astronomically it tells me that there are millions of galaxies and potentially billions of planets. Astrologically it tells me that Saturn is in Leo. Horologically it tells me that it's about quarter to three in the morning. Meteorologically it tells me that tomorrow will probably be a beautiful day. And theologically it tells me that we are but a small part of the great whole."

He stopped for a moment. "What does it tell you, Holmes?"

"Watson, you idiot," replied he, "it means that someone has stolen our tent."

Now maybe you've heard this before, and it is indeed funny but more than that it's highly instructive for us in regard to JKD precisely because we are often no better than Watson at discerning the plain facts before our eyes. There are, of course, a multitude of interpretations of JKD around and I think that many of them fail in precisely this fashion - they overcomplicate the issue and render us blind to the obvious facts before our very eyes.

We are presently living in a time of rapid and mind-numbing change. Sure, every generation must deal with the previous one regaling them with stories of hardship and scarcity. That such is a common refrain doesn't make it less true that those of us living today have luxuries that previous generations could not have imagined. I mean to call your attention to this at the start of a book about martial arts in general and Jeet Kune Do in particular because how we think about life and history has a very direct impact on our understanding of Bruce Lee's fighting method.

There is alive in the minds of all us a certain bias against the past. C.S. Lewis coined it chronological snobbery, which is to say that those of us living in the present will always, and rather naturally, assume that we're smarter than those rubes that lived in the past. This is especially true here in America where we have the materialistic concept of the American Dream - namely that we'll be better off than our parents - drilled into us from a young age. It's our birthright it would seem. And who can argue with this logic because, after all, I'm typing this on a wireless keyboard and my father typed on a manual typewriter. Oh, the horror! And I haven't seen whiteout in years, thank God.

In the avalanche of time and the hurried business of our days it's regrettably easy to lose our place in history. In America, as in most of the West, families are scattered and torn, so our comprehension of Self in relation to the past is tenuous if not altogether eradicated. Worse still, schools rarely teach history except to pass judgment on all those bigots, racists, and war-mongers of the past. The system seems to tell us with one voice, "We're better than that, now." We are the future we've been waiting for, if I may paraphrase a recent line from a famous politician.

During the student protests in the 60's, Ronald Reagan, then governor of California, agreed to meet with some of the so-called protest leaders. They came into his office and there was a stark contrast between the already aged Reagan and the scraggly, hippie, unshaven students. The student groups were claiming that the universities of California were really, truly their property—the people's. So they had sitins and demonstrations and basically ground the normal functions of the colleges to a smelly, hairy halt. Asked to give an account of their right to do such things, the leader excoriated Governor Reagan.

"When you were born, old man, there weren't jet airplanes...no radios, no cars..."

All of this was true. His point, the climax of his pugnacious and chronologically snobbish diatribe, was that Reagan's time and ideas had passed. The Governor, untroubled by this scornful lambasting, simply agreed with the young revolutionary.

"You're right," he said serenely. "You're right...my generation made these things, son, and gave them to you. Now I suggest that you go home, take a bath, shave, put on some real clothes and get a job so that maybe you can produce something someday too."

You see, the protester's logic was as bad as his hygiene. And he can be forgiven, as many can be today, for drawing the conclusion that the past was irrelevant—swept away by the oceans of time, technology and progress. What did Reagan's generation have to say of consequence to him? His own education, like ours, saw the past as something to be repealed, perhaps atoned for, not learned from. But it's a dreadful thing to politicize history because we got here from there and to treat yesterday without humility and circumspection is to court the disasters that pride is wed to.

Most people in 1900 America never traveled more than 12 miles from home because that was about the distance a horse would take you in a day. Travel by stagecoach was still common and it was so bumpy, dusty, and nasty that Mark Twain said of it that he needed an unabridged dictionary to properly express his joy when the trip was finally, mercifully over. That the first car to ever cross the continental United States, from San Francisco to New York, did so in 1903 is astonishing considering how ubiquitous car travel is today. That it took nearly two months of unimaginable endurance, mechanical know-how, and blind optimism to accomplish the feat is also telling. Today we drive at incredible speeds, in pure luxury, and on wonderfully paved roads (save a pothole or two).

Or let us consider the year of Bruce Lee's birth, 1940. Not only was the world soon to be enslaved by that most hideous atrocity, World War II, but life was still so dangerous in other ways too. America had a crippled president—stricken by a disease, polio, that we need not fear anymore. Smallpox was still scarring, blinding, and killing. Hundreds of thousands of people, even in the advanced countries, still died from simple infections. A few years before Lee's birth, President Coolidge's own son died after contracting an infection from playing tennis on the White House grounds. Yes, indeed, even the richest and most powerful people in the world couldn't escape the harshness of everyday life.

When I told my son recently that when I was his age if the Yankees played a game on the West coast on a Wednesday night that I, living in New York, wouldn't know the score until Friday morning, he looked confounded.

"Why?" he asked in his 7 year-old innocence. "What did you do?"

"What do you mean?"

"You got in trouble?"

My son's perplexity at this was both humorous and shocking. It simply never occurred to him that my only source of news was the newspaper and that a game ending at 1AM Eastern time wouldn't make the morning deadline. Therefore, unless I caught the evening sports, which I never did because the TV was off during dinner or mom had thrown us out of the house to play, I had to wait until the next day's newspaper. My son, with ESPN, smartphones, and satellite radio, simply couldn't conceive of not finding whatever information he wanted right when he wanted it. Quite naturally he then assumed that I must have gotten grounded or something (a manifest impossibility, that, since I was a blessed angel for my entire childhood).

What this has to do with Jeet Kune Do and Bruce Lee is that we must understand and respect the old if we are to fully comprehend Lee's method. That's right: JKD is nothing new at all; it's simply the old...the old that's been forgotten and overlooked. Our bias against history leaves us at a significant disadvantage in apprehending Lee's real genius because we start from a flawed presupposition. JKD isn't new, it is simply a combination of old-school boxing and Wing Chun.

Now, of course, if you're conditioned as a chronological snob you'll likely resent this assessment, but none of the evidence will much help your case. Should you wish to dispute my contention you will do well to steer clear of Lee's actual work. The Tao of Jeet Kune Do, for instance, is almost entirely Lee's repackaging of the boxing masters. To read it is to read the past the likes of Dempsey and Driscoll. Without boxing there would be no Tao of Jeet Kune Do as we know it.

There is, also, that first bias—Watson's error—that we should be exceedingly wary of: the anti-simplicity bias. I have often encountered high-ranking martial artists that have told me that boxing is of little use in real fighting. It only has four punches, they state flatly as if they have just uttered a truth so resounding, an argument so impregnable that only a fool would utter a word in dispute. In this, they've wrapped their disdain for the simple but true in a warm blanket of historical ignorance, for boxing always was a self-defense method - one tested, tested, and tested again. To see boxing as only a sport—not taking it's lessons and applying them, as Lee did, to the larger context of all-out fighting—is to out of hand reject over two thousand years of very refined fistic truth.

So, to carry either of these two biases forward in our examination of Mr. Lee's JKD, or worse, to embrace both of them, will invariably cause us to miss his genius altogether. We'll delve more deeply into the nuts and bolts of JKD's unique combination of Wing Chun (simple and refined) and boxing (historical and bare-fisted) but I thought it was most important to address these issues first as I believe that they lay at the root of much of our confusion in regard to JKD.

To be sure, Bruce Lee was a great and gifted man but he was not some infallible martial deity. He came to America right in the early stages of his Wing Chun training and, though he was extraordinarily talented and diligent, he was certainly no Wing Chun master at 18 years-old. Thus, decades from Skype, Facetime and YouTube, when faced with his own limitations of a system he hadn't fully learned, the young Lee simply extrapolated on the principles he knew to be true from WC and saw their cousin in the old-school boxing system. This is the raw material that he worked with and, therefore, it's the same material we should offer students so that they have the opportunity to see and experience it for themselves.

And because of his untimely demise, we never witnessed Mr. Lee get older. We never saw him have a cinematic flop as he was cut down while his career was ascending. But he was mere flesh and blood that rose on the disciplines of Wing Chun Kuen and Western boxing. Yes, yes...Mr. Lee was a unique combination of East and West and so it was with his fighting method too. It's my earnest belief that if we understand, teach and train JKD from this historically true and simple perspective then we'll equip another generation to meet and even surpass him. Frankly, if I didn't believe this was possible I wouldn't run a school of my own. The following is the underlying theory and technical basics of the Jeet Kune Do that I teach at our Academy. Future volumes will explore training practices, sparring, and chi-sao, and, yes, the rest of the Wing Chun system that Lee was never able to learn.

Lastly, as already implied, there are clear and systemic likenesses between the Wing Chun method and traditional boxing that we should understand and respect. I would like to suggest that these two methods compliment each other in such a fashion as to give us a robust application method we can then call Jeet Kune Do and we can do this without savaging either system.

It isn't my contention here that this is the only way to go about JKD. It is, though, my belief that it's within this context—and the truth, to paraphrase Cornelius Van Til, is somewhere in this area so we should know where to look. It is my express intent, however, to give this historical perspective to the JKD debate and to try and train up another generation of men and women who can carry on this method. Martial arts has been a great blessing for me in my life and it is something that I love to share with all that I can. I truly do believe that all people can benefit from the proper study of this simple, effective and scientific approach to self-defense.

Also, a quick word of thanks to the many individuals that have greatly assisted and instructed me on my martial journey of over 30 years. I can truly say that I thank God for these disciplines that have shaped my life because they have afforded me the opportunity to meet, train with, learn from, and even become friends with some very great people.

Sifu Lamar Davis has been a tireless supporter of Wing Chun's importance to Jeet Kune Do for a great many years and without him it's likely that an entire generation of JKD students would have lost Wing Chun entirely. I've had the benefit of training with him many times over the last 22 years, having first met him in September of 1991. In all of that time he has never wavered in his devotion to preserving the historical reality of Bruce Lee's JKD.

My kung-fu brother, Jonathan Parsons deserves some special mention as he's been a true friend for many years. Not only did Jonathan introduce me to his Sifu, Ted Wong, in 1995 but he went out of his way to see to it that I might benefit greatly from the late instructor's knowledge.

As it went, Jonathan was bringing Sifu Wong in for a seminar in Upstate

New York in the autumn of 1995 which I enthusiastically planned to attend. My dear friend called me a few weeks before hand, though, and made me a shocking offer.

"What are you doing the week before the seminar?" he asked.

"Working," I replied matter-of-factly.

"Well," he said, "Sifu is coming in on Sunday."

"He's coming in after the seminar starts?"

I'm a little slow sometimes, it would appear.

"No," he laughed. "He's coming in the weekend before and he's staying the whole week."

"Wow," was all I could manage to say as I wrestled with jealousy quietly in my heart. I couldn't dream of doing something like that at that time. I was 25. My school consisted of maybe 10 students and I was working full-time for a delivery service called Airborne Express (imagine FedEx without the good pay, benefits and on-time percentage). "That's awesome," I uttered weakly.

"Well, Jay," he said, "can you come up?"

"Yeah. I'll be there for the seminar."

"No," he laughed again at my cluelessness. "Can you come in for the week to train with him? You can stay in the spare bedroom."

"Jonathan...Jonathan...I can't afford that. I can barely afford to get up there," I said, because I was in South Carolina.

"I'm not asking you to pay. It's all set. Sifu's gonna be here the whole week and I've got some other things to do here and there, so you can train with him and pick his brain."

Silence.

"What do you think? Can you do it?"

I remember going to my boss, Phil, at Airborne Express the next day and telling him that I needed the entire next week off.

"You can't..."

"I know...I know," I agreed. "I don't expect you to let me but I've got to go." I explained the situation and said, "...if I don't have a job when I get back, I don't blame you but I've got to do this. This is what I love."

Well, Phil was a heck of a nice guy and was, apparently, a closet dreamer himself, so he let me go without firing me. It was an unpaid week off but that's all it cost—obviously the economy was a bit better back then. So I went to spend the week to get free private classes all day at my friend's expense. If you've been around martial arts long enough you know that egos and insecurity are rampant and such behavior is rare.

It was during this week that Sifu Wong opened up Bruce Lee's boxing roots to me. Always uncomfortable in front of large crowds and not much liking attention, he truly thrived in a more personal environment like this. We discussed the boxing masters of the past over bagels and coffee, and he explained Bruce's emphasis on footwork, straight hitting and timing as the foundation of simplicity while we stood in the parking lot off route 50. That was our classroom. Great blessings come from great friends and I owe both Jonathan and Ted Wong my deepest appreciation for all that they did for me during a time when often the only currency I had to trade was my enthusiasm and, according to Sifu Wong, my sense of humor.

My Wing Chun Sifu, Tony Massengill, also deserves a special mention and heartfelt thanks for making this work possible. Sifu Tony's knowledge of the Ip Man Wing Chun system is utterly astonishing. He's an ideas man, a gifted communicator who truly, truly desires that his students get better than him. Last year he said to me that if when he dies none of his students are better than he is then, in fact, he's left Wing Chun weaker through his instruction. How many instructors truly live this code? It's a rare thing, indeed. I've never been around an instructor who takes such joy in teaching and watching his students get better and I'm absolutely blessed to have met him and become his student. In fact, it was Sifu Tony who really helped me to understand that many of the strengths of JKD were really Wing Chun concepts after all and this revolutionized the way I see and teach at my school.

Lastly, I must give my deepest thanks to all those at Greenville Academy of Martial Arts. We have such a wondrous, blessed family of gifted martial artists here that I can never go home in a bad mood. Iron sharpens iron.

Aaron Bouchillon and Mark Strickland are both full instructors in JKD and Wing Chun and are two of the best men I have ever known.

Kacy Hatmaker, an assistant JKD instructor who is working hard at Wing Chun, Jesse Moshure an Academy JKD and Wing Chun instructor, and Jazilyn Wiley, one of our top young students, are also featured here. Jeff Hatmaker is also shown—often getting punched and for that we apologize…he's much better than the photos would imply. MMA amateur champion Caleb Savage (no kidding on the last name) is also shown.

A special, special thank you is also extended to my friend and student, James Schoeni, who contributed most of the photos for this book. James has the true heart (and eye) of an artist and it was because of conversations with him that I decided to use photographs that weren't dry, technical and posed. We wanted to show you a little of the dynamic that we experience every night at our school as people train and talk and learn. For this I owe James a great, great debt of gratitude.

It's because of people like these that our school is such a magical place and it's what I imagined kung-fu schools should be when I was a young man dreaming of not working a "real" job. We're a family here and I wish to all the readers and devotees to our discipline the same type of friendship, sweat, wisdom, laughter and love that we experience here.

Thank you for reading,

Jason Korol
Greenville, South Carolina
August 2013

JEET KUNE DO

First things first

The first thing to be said about JKD is that, quite sadly, it's a veritable mess. And this is nearly tragic because it has so many great benefits to offer students seeking a real world self-defense method. The primary cause of this mess, I believe, is improper definitions of the nature of Bruce Lee's fighting method. My claim that JKD is simply a stylistic variation of Wing Chun cuts through the tangled mess that these distorted definitions have wrought upon us. I will offer a short survey of the technical points of this approach later in the book—not meant to be exhaustive but to at least assist the reader in having a mental image to connect to the ideas.

There are basically two approaches to teaching JKD today and they each stem from the teacher's philosophical starting point in reference to the method. This is the first point that we must get right: a man's presupposition, his philosophy, is the central thing out of which everything grows. If we start with a flawed presupposition we cannot arrive at the truth. These other methods are in fact competing philosophies and I will address them from that standpoint.

The first we'll look at against our own belief that JKD is Lee's unique combination of old-school boxing and Wing Chun, is what's known as JKD Concepts. The Concepts approach, as it's called, is ruled by the opinion that Lee himself didn't see JKD as a particular thing to be practiced but as an idea to be applied to practice. The problem rears its head immediately, though, when one rather naturally asks, "Okay, what's the idea?" A clear answer is never quite forthcoming. Instead, we'll hear discussions and lectures on things like "doing your own thing" and "being more efficient" and the like. But these are hardly a grand, unifying, directing idea that can be applied to practice. In fact, they are ideas that people at high levels have always had in every field. Are we to believe that before Bruce Lee no one ever studied their martial art with an eye to becoming more practical? It would seem, at least to a casual observer, that Muhammad Ali, without ever having met the Little Dragon had done these things quite well all by himself, so calling these ideas Jeet Kune Do is a bit of a stretch.

In Concepts circles there is much talk of how Bruce Lee studied many different methods to arrive at his own personal "jeet kune do" and, consequently, this must be taken into the motley mix of concepts that make up the Jeet Kune Do Concepts. They go so far as to say that Lee studied 26 different methods to make up his own. The thought here being that this is the process, the concept, that marks the JKD man or woman…the researching of other already existing methods to draw up one's own personal JKD.

Yet this is all rather fanciful and illogical. It's fanciful because there's no evidence anywhere of Bruce Lee ever saying such a thing. This whole 26 different styles business was brought to everyone's attention by one of his students years after Lee's untimely passing. One would think that if it was so integral a part of his own philosophy that he would have told more people and/or written about it extensively. But from JKD's founder we have not a peep. Two private students of Lee's, Ted Wong and Joe Lewis, when I asked them about this directly, both stated emphatically that they never heard Lee mention that he had researched a specific number of other systems in order to arrive at the fistic truths he was teaching them. The truth, they said, was quite the opposite—Lee told them of JKD's boxing/fencing/Wing Chun roots.

The intellectual father of the Concepts movement is Dan Inosanto. In his first book about JKD, "Jeet Kune Do: the Art and Philosophy of

Bruce Lee," Inosanto actually includes a chapter called, "Wing Chun: the Nucleus." We should note carefully that there is no chapter titled, "The 26 arts: the Nucleus." Moreover, the vast majority of the training photos are of boxing drills and Wing Chun style practice. To be sure, these are the same things that students do at my school today under the direction of our philosophy that JKD is an old school boxing/Wing Chun vehicle.

Worse still is how illogical the whole business is. If Lee actually did develop his method from the study of these fabulous 26 methods, why aren't Concepts students doing the same? And what was the common thread of these 26 arts—what did they all have in common that Lee studied them? And, while we're at it, why not 27 arts...or 30...or 50? There are no good answers for these questions from Concepts instructors because in reality there are none.

Perhaps the Concepts approach is telling us that the root is in the very action of studying other methods? Well, if this were so then every professor and student in world history has been doing Jeet Kune Do since they routinely read and research. Every history researcher... every Christian who reads the Koran and vice versa...every Taco Bell executive who studies Burger King.

Lastly, if this is indeed it—that the nebulous and evasive Concept of JKD is really research—why all the fuss about lineage and certification? Any Tae Kwon Do black belt who reads about other methods can be said to be a JKD Concepts instructor if this is true. But such cross-training and research has been going on for thousands of years throughout history. It's called trade, innovation, research, etc. So, if this is Lee's great idea, methinks it's a rather strange "great" idea to be credited with, like a man running around with a wheel and exclaiming, "See!"

Interestingly enough, our approach actually rescues JKD from the Concepts mess by clearly defining Lee's method. It actually *is* a system of concepts. Yes, I agree, that Lee's JKD is a method rooted and founded upon concepts. But these concepts are Wing Chun concepts.

My assertion is not—I'd like to be as clear as possible on this point—that Concepts students and teachers are incompetent hacks. Many, I am sure, are tremendous martial artists in their own right, owing to great dedication and training. Many have immersed themselves in Muay Thai and Brazilian Jujitsu, which are formidable systems not to be toyed with in any respect. Honorable and splendid though they might be, however, these systems are not precisely JKD…they are either Muay Thai or BJJ and that is what the Concepts student/ teacher has, in fact, mastered. That is the root of their skill. Their skill is no different than other Muay Thai or BJJ experts. To say otherwise is to demean those systems, as if to say that they could not possibly have produced men capable of mastering and applying them—which is patently absurd. But the patently absurd is exactly what JKD Concepts produces as a logical consequence of its faulty, ill-defined premise.

A JKD that understands its origins, that it grew out of Wing Chun and that Wing Chun is itself an extraordinarily unique system of concepts, is a JKD that can be taught, comprehended and, indeed, grow. It needs to be understood, though, that Wing Chun is not, repeat not, a knuckle-headed system enslaved to the straight blast or any other Wing Chun-looking technique. Rather, its forms are moving textbooks of structures, principles, and strategies designed to be absorbed and used by the student. Properly understood, Wing Chun is not a static gathering of technique and sticking hands any more than Jimi Hendrix, with a guitar in his hands, was a guy with six strings, chords and the scales. Of course, that's who he was, if you have a very fixed, wooden way of percieving him. However, Jimi was, as the Wing Chun master strives to be, a man that had mastered those concepts and structures (for that is what they are, like the Wing Chun forms), and made them his own. Like the guitarist, the Wing Chun master uses the ideas and structures of the forms to express himself in fighting; he is not used by them but is their master, not their slave. That many practitioners never reach this level of superlative skill is not proof that Wing Chun doesn't work, just as we still listen to our favorite music though hacks far outnumber talented artists.

So, in this point the Concepts students have it right: JKD is an ideas based method. Where they err is in not understanding that these ideas are found within the Wing Chun system. Other systems have forms that are imaginary fighting scenarios. Wing Chun forms are no such thing. The mistake is in looking at the movements in the Wing Chun forms and drawing a hyper-literal interpretation from them—missing the conceptual/structural basis that the movements are expressing—and then declaring the system wanting. Well! This is exactly what the Concepts group does. They are right to understand Lee's point that the method (JKD) is conceptual, but they run off into the intellectual wilderness chasing ghosts when they miss the obvious.

Most can be forgiven, we must concede, for believing that Lee had dumped his ex-art and moved on to the more brilliantly beautiful and useful JKD because of the myths surrounding Lee's early Wing Chun days. What are these myths exactly? Well, for one, most of us in JKD have been fed that line that Lee was a master or near-master of the system when he arrived on the American continent in 1959. To the contrary, first-hand accounts from people that would know, like Duncan Leung, place Bruce's training at only 2 to 3 years in duration between the ages of 16 and18. He was not training every waking moment of every day as some Westerners like to believe, as if the Chinese live in some kind of perpetual Kung-fu theatre dreamland—Kung-fu all the time! Parenthetically, we have the same bias in reverse for America due to the export of our movies that make many foreigners believe all we do here is have sex and chase our whims and no one works for a living. But at any rate, young Bruce Lee was quite involved in activities besides Wing Chun.

To start, he was in school. Also, he was a child actor and was usually filming before school hours. They did this because to film after the pre-dawn was nearly impossible due to the noise of Hong Kong streets. Lee also was such a talented dancer that he won a cha-cha competition in 1958. I'm not a dancer but one assumes that winning a dance competition would have required a bit of practice. Also, it was an excellent way to spend time with girls, another favorite thing for young Bruce. And, finally, he trained for, competed in and emerged victorious in a boxing competition.

Now, this isn't to say that JKD's founder wasn't serious about his Wing Chun training but it should put things in their proper context. He wasn't doing private classes around the clock. He was a teenage boy with a variety of interests and responsibilities and, no, Ip Man was not giving him private classes every day either. For goodness sake, the late grandmaster was eligible for AARP membership when Lee started. How many men of that age spend all of their time with teenage boys save for Jerry Sandusky?

So, when Lee's ship docked in America, he stepped off as a very talented Wing Chun student, but he was far from a master of the system. His chief mentor back in Hong Kong, Wong Shun Leung, was the true fighting champion of the Wing Chun clan—undefeated in dozens of "beimo" matches (rooftop skill comparisons). Had Wong landed in America and started teaching that would have been different, but this was an 18-year-old young man who, if lucky, had learned half of the system of Wing Chun. Quite naturally, there were limitations to what our young leader knew and could do with his fighting method, so he trained and taught a modified version of it. Nevertheless, it was still steeped in Wing Chun concepts like simplicity, directness, straight hitting, etc.

Then there is the famous match with Wong Jak Man. As JKD people tell it, Lee won the fight but was discouraged by his performance. He was winded (how is that Wing Chun's fault?) and he didn't possess "stopping" power and adaptability to his foe's hit and run tactics. Not in any rendering of the fight that I've heard has it been mentioned that Lee was ever in danger of losing, which is quite a feat for a young man with his training background considering that the Chinatown leaders that challenged him likely put their best fighter forward. Still, though, Lee had trouble finishing the challenger due to his longer range strikes and evasive tactics (some say he was actually running away at times).

Let's pause for a moment and consider a few critical points that this altercation brings forth.

First, Lee's Wing Chun obviously wasn't so ineffective that it cost him the fight. He won handily but exhibited some tactical limitations that bugged him. Afterwards he was fanatical about his physical conditioning as he was so winded from the long encounter that he could barely punch by the end of it. But his having to chase down a running opponent might be seen in different light if we remember that Wing Chun isn't a competitive method but, rather, a selfdefense method. In a real fight, not a match, if your opponent is running away, you've won. There's no reason to have to finish him... you're safe. In this case, absent the demands of the bout (that the loser had to submit or be stopped), Lee's Wing Chun worked rather handily. Therefore, considering this bout to be an example of how Wing Chun doesn't really work is foolish. It worked perfectly. The problem was the event was a match rather than a fight. That Lee wanted to improve on his performance is one thing; to say that he needed to change his method is another thing altogether.

Secondly, it's hard not to imagine that Lee's inexperience played a role in his "poor" performance as well. What would have happened to Wong Jak Man had he confronted a prime Ip Man or, for that matter, Wong Shun Leung? Bruce Lee was not the best fighter of the Wing Chun clan yet he easily bested the Chinatown community's chosen representative. Had he been more seasoned perhaps the outcome would have been more satisfactory for him. Of course, we can't know that for certain but we do know that Lee's training had been incomplete and afterwards he was honest enough with himself to admit that he wasn't as good as he could be. There was no way for him to go back to Hong Kong at that time and finish his training and he was decades away from the internet and DVD's. In short, his fistic education in Wing Chun Kuen was at a dead-end for all intent and purposes. To grow he needed to expand his studies.

This brings us to our third point regarding the fight. There's no evidence anywhere of Lee toying around with different methods after the fight. Obviously, he continued to develop the consequences of his theories and principles, but he saw old-school, Jim Driscoll/Jack Dempsey boxing as the key to expanding on the Wing Chun foundation that he knew worked. For example, he knew that simplicity was key, and straight hitting, intercepting, and adaptability (having no way as way) were integral points of proper combat theory. These were Wing Chun ideas and they were shared by old-school boxing. Moreover, Lee knew that his mentor back in Hong Kong, Wong Shun Leung, had been a boxer before he devoted himself to Wing Chun. Wong had been so good that when he first came to Ip Man's school he easily beat a few students while using boxing. It wasn't until he was beaten (with difficulty) by a top student and then handled with superior skill and control by the grandmaster himself that he dropped boxing and became a disciple of the venerable Ip Man.

Boxing's straight lead, mobile power, long range capability, and emphasis on sparring to develop distance and timing were the perfect tonic to what ailed Lee. Thus, JKD was born. There's no evidence that Lee changed his operational system—his core concepts—just that he adjusted his training and application habits. Thus (and I will return to this point throughout the book) Lee's JKD became a "style" of Wing Chun. The Floyd Mayweather style of boxing is vastly different than the Mike Tyson style, but they are both doing the method of boxing. Bruce Lee's JKD for all intent and purposes was basically a style of the Wing Chun concept/method.

Also, and lastly on this point, the challenge itself stemmed from the fact that Lee was teaching non-Chinese. It's easy to think in America that we're the only people that have racial issues but everyone always has and, sadly it seems, always will. The Chinese didn't much appreciate Bruce teaching Chinese kung-fu to Westerners and, like Taky Kimura, the Japanese. But Lee saw only people, not race. He taught women, blacks, whoever wanted to learn. This is interesting and should be noted by those JKD instructors today that insist that you can't teach JKD to children. Lee never put limitations on the human spirit and its desire to learn and grow. Naturally, this put him at odds with the old guard.

This is also instructive in the way that Lee integrated Wing Chun and boxing. He was interested in the truth, the whole truth, and nothing but the truth. If he saw something that worked, he didn't care where it came from—he used it. In this event he crossed a boundary many from the East, bound by tradition, never dare to cross. He challenged tradition with the truth. Lee was a man between two nations and cultures. He was Chinese and yet he was American. The two played off of each other. He understood the principles and structure of Wing Chun, and yet he loved the testing and freedom of Western boxing. He respected the past but wasn't bound by it. In the East you had a role, a place, and that was your lot; in America it was about what you could do. Lee was East and West and so was his Jeet Kune Do. It was principled pragmatism, for without principle there is no way to know why something did or did not work. Lee didn't care where you came from or who your parents were—he cared about the heart and soul of the human being. For this reason he's still rightly admired and he's a unique bridge between two great cultures. These cultural influences clashed that day of the fight and afterwards Lee moved to further embrace the Westerner in him because he had to. It had already been in him, on the outskirts of his philosophy and practice, but the match with the oldguard crystalized it for him in a concrete, physical manner. But, again, his creation was nothing that his Wing Chun principles hadn't already intimated to him. After all, what does it mean to "make Wing Chun your slave" but to truly understand and integrate its principles and structure so that one expresses those things freely, as needed?

A Concepts instructor that doesn't understand all of this might know in his heart that Lee was talking about principles, but he can never apprehend those ideas and in turn communicate them to his students. This is the problem of JKD Concepts. They must always cannibalize existing systems.

The other approach, known as Original JKD, is like a body without a head. It grew as a response to the ubiquitous nature of JKD

Concepts in the '80's. Now I must say, by way of disclosure, that I've spent the vast majority of my training time with Original instructors. In offering up a critique of Original philosophy it isn't my intent to savage anyone, much less those men that shared their knowledge with me. The same goes with the Concepts approach as, like everyone else that trained in JKD in the '80's, I was reared under that philosophy since it was the only one around until Ted Wong and Lamar Davis (most notably) came forward with the Original concept.

Original JKD focuses on material that Bruce Lee actually did during his lifetime. Frustrated by the Inosanto-led way of training Filipino methods while talking about Bruce Lee, this movement attracted many who saw the Concepts way as erroneous and wanted to do the more Wing Chun based JKD that they'd seen Lee practice. Of course, this set off quite a political firestorm back in the '90's. In any event, the Original movement picked up quite a head of steam despite vigorous and sordid attempts by its enemies to stamp it out. Insofar as a person trains in Original JKD, they have two primary paths to follow. The one is in training under an instructor that learned from Lee personally and is simply passing along that material to his students. The other is in training with a Sifu that has an integrated curriculum of Lee's teaching from his schools in Seattle, Oakland and L.A. Chinatown.

As far as intellectual integrity goes, there is nothing to criticize in an instructor who learned under Bruce Lee and in turn passes on to eager students what the Little Dragon taught him. The work of a multitude of former Lee students like Jesse Glover and Ted Wong (to name but two) has been exactly like this. Naturally, all of these instructors modified their approach a bit as the years passed—personalized it, if you will—but they basically stayed true to the mechanics and spirit of the material Lee taught them.

My experience with Ted Wong is an instructive example. When I trained with him in the mid-90's he was still teaching some basic trapping movements such as pak-sao and lop-sao. As the years passed, however, it became clear that he was less and less enamored with Wing Chun elements in JKD. A year before he passed away we had a conversation about this where he told me that he saw this as a natural evolution of an intercepting fist method that emphasized movement, long-range fire power, and simplicity above all else. He was, though, forever a humble, humble man and never claimed that this was the only way of looking at things—just that he thought it was the most logical progression in a method that stressed simplicity and aliveness.

There were similar issues with other former Lee students as well. Jesse Glover, for example, began teaching what he called Non-Classical Gung-fu, which went the opposite direction of Ted Wong—Glover working his material more on the inside and Wong on the outside. And both of these men trained from the same instructor, so you can see just from this how Original JKD has its own unique problems.

On the other hand, we have instructors that purport to teach a form of unadulterated JKD, pure JKD or some such thing. The vast majority of these instructors did not train personally with Lee but, rather, studied to a varying degree under his students. Lamar Davis, for example, has been certified under instructors from the different "eras" of Lee's teaching: Seattle (highly Wing Chun orientated), Oakland (a little less Wing Chun) and Los Angeles (more long range and far less Wing Chun). With this pedigree Sifu Davis teaches his brand of JKD with all the confidence and tenacity as if JKD was the gospel and he was the Apostle Paul minus the appearance of Bruce on Damascus Road. But instructors like Lamar Davis have a far more difficult job in that they are burdened with trying to determine what parts of Lee's teaching require more and less focus than others. Most of the students of these "pure" JKD instructors that I've seen all look identical—carbon copy students with their stances mirror images of their instructors. How is this possible when Lee's own students didn't exhibit this? If what these men are teaching is pure, then why didn't Jesse Glover and Ted Wong have the same stance? The only answer—by their own definition—is that Lee himself wasn't teaching pure JKD.

This "pure" JKD approach, without Wing Chun and boxing at its core, absolutely has to run into problems like this: if Lee's JKD is about scientific street-fighting, why was Lee teaching Joe Lewis how to compete in tournaments? We know that Lee was irritated when his champion student, on top of the competitive karate world of his day, identified his art not as JKD but as his native karate style. What was it that Lewis used to dominate the full-contact world of his day? Was it not "JKD Concepts" of simplicity, broken rhythm, set-point control (with faking and countering), scientific footwork, and the educated use of the lead hand and foot? Yes, indeed. This is what Lee taught Joe Lewis—one of the finest competitive full-contact fighters of all-time. Lee taught him the concepts and applications of JKD that he had ingeniously borrowed and organized from Wing Chun and old-style boxing (heavy as it was with fencing strategy which worked wonderfully in competitions and tournaments, by the way).

This is the honest mistake that such Original instructors run into and why I believe that our approach is the right one since it is able to make sense of such otherwise vexing issues. I must pause again to say that I am in no way claiming that these instructors are all hacks. I'm sure there are some. That is irrelevant to our point. Our issue is with the philosophy of the whole thing and how current Original JKD philosophy is fundamentally flawed and will end up, in the long run, killing the very thing it loves.

With the problems of the Concepts group already articulated, they did at least hold true in one philosophical respect: that fighting is done by an individual, not a style and the individual must be free to explore, adapt and grow. In short, where the Concepts group fails in never accurately defining the big concept, they do succeed in not enslaving the student to the art/ teacher. The Original movement, however, is a philosophical nightmare when it makes what Bruce Lee was doing— or worse—Bruce Lee himself, the process and goal of training.

We must again omit many first generation students from this particular critique in that they were/are merely sharing what they were taught without being burdened by the larger context. The goal of the larger Original movement has morphed past these men, though, into an art all by itself and it's this that I mean to address and illuminate its malignant shortcomings. Still, though, I pause in my critique to state again that I am merely—for the sake of truth—offering these observations. That I'm pointing out perceived irrationality and contradictions in these approaches is not to say that those teaching or following them are evil or incompetent.

And what contradiction is at the heart of the Original movement? Well, simply put it's that Lee wasn't teaching a new thing but a combination of existing methods. These methods were Ip Man Wing Chun and boxing. An attempt to teach "original" JKD without really delving into these methods enslaves the student in a pathetic cycle of "Bruce did this, then he did that…and then this…"

Well, let's all buy a yellow track suit, marry a woman

named Linda, get a big dog named Bobo...

The Original movement collapses in on itself (as Concepts people will agree) because it holds Lee up to be an idol. All hail Saint Bruce who freed us from the classical mess. But to focus on what he did without reference to the broader systems prohibits us from understanding *why* he did what he did, and we exchange one slave master for another. If an Original JKD instructor is teaching trapping he's actually teaching Wing Chun concepts and structures but he's not giving his students the full benefit of them. In most cases he doesn't know the whole Wing Chun system himself so the student has no way of really knowing the heart of the movements and he becomes a slave to the system.

My contention, of course, is that JKD is a Wing Chun based system, a unique combination of Wing Chun and old-school boxing. Therefore, it logically follows that all JKD instruction should be done by instructors steeped in those methods or else students will only receive modifications made by one talented man (Lee) and never learn the source. Our approach is that JKD is a conceptual art and the concepts are Wing Chun concepts so we should teach Wing Chun while showing Lee's unique training and application interpretations (borrowed heavily from boxing) so that the student can make their own necessary modifications. Modifications are necessary because every individual must take the material and apply it for themselves. Methods do not fight on their own, and a student that understands this and integrates into reflexive action the core concepts of these systems can become their master, not their slave; they will serve him, not the other way around. This, I believe, is the true "original" method.

The other major contradiction of Original JKD, like its counterpart, JKD Concepts, is that it stumbles over the issue of certification. All of the bickering over who certified who and whatnot is as detrimental as it is illogical. If we have, as I believe we should, future JKD instructors certified through a lineage that runs back to Ip Man, we can do away with a whole mess of problems.

Let's remember that Lee himself was never qualified to teach Wing Chun. Consequently, anyone certified by Lee is certified to teach by a man who wasn't certified. This isn't to say that their knowledge of correct concepts and ability to apply them is fraudulent, just that Lee had no true certification himself.

Moreover, we get back to the root of the problem. What is JKD? If it's not Wing Chun based old-school boxing then what exactly is it? If you say that it's Jun Fan Gung-fu then you'resaying that it's modified Wing Chun and—think about this—it's really just a modified version of a system a young man never finished for himself. In short, it's a modified version of half a system.

By returning to the root systems that are obvious for all to see we can escape these conundrums once and for all. To eschew this approach leaves us mired in a series of hopeless contradictions. Again—since Lee wasn't a master of the Wing Chun system that he modified why shouldn't we teach students that very system so that they can see for themselves if the modifications are valid or not?

This fact (of Lee not being ertified) is undisputed and lies waste to the claims of those that build their reputation on being certified by this and that Bruce Lee student. It might be all well and good that you are certified by every Bruce Lee student to ever have drawn a breath but what exactly did he (Lee) certify them to teach? And what of all those certifications floating around by men who weren't certified by Lee? I've met and trained with some of these original Lee students that weren't certified themselves and for the most part they were just doing the best they could with a difficult situation. After all, when Lee died there was a great clamor to know all things that he'd done. Suddenly these men were in great demand. There was no order, no hierarchical structure to guide teachers and students so I'm not saying that these men were greedy manipulators though some have and still do exist. I think, rather, what happened in the extreme cases was that the passion and enthusiasm of some men overcame their skill and logic.

When Lee died and the hordes flocked to his students there was a dreadful vacuum and I think that, for the most part, his former students were stuck in a most difficult bind. Most of them knew that they weren't taught a workable system that they could teach others. Lee wasn't that kind of teacher—he gave people bits and pieces of his brilliance, he inspired as much or more than he actually taught in some cases. But how could they transform this into a working system in order to teach? What was the curriculum to be? How could you rank students and how could you gauge if a student was ready to teach others? Worse still, many biases were taken on with no thought whatsoever such as not recognizing—as other systems do—advanced practitioners but only teachers. Imagine for a moment the insanity of every black belt in every system being a teacher too, or every graduate of college being designated a professor.

This mayhem has continued to this day with many students toiling away to become instructors only because there is no other advanced rank available to them. The alternative is to offer "rank" or belts and this, think many in JKD/Wing Chun circles, automatically makes "belt factories" and belt factories are the lowest rung of hell in their minds. Instead of thinking for themselves—logically—they hear that Lee didn't like organized systems and schools so they determine that his was a voice speaking from heaven and that, consequently, all workings of successful martial arts schools must therefore be evil. If you don't like Tae Kwon Do that's one thing, but there is no denying that they run good schools. And this nonsense of Lee having a "secret" kwoon (school) is utter foolishness. Bruce Lee gave the largest JKD class in history on the Longstreet episode and he was a master of marketing, a consummate showman, and, of course, a major motion picture star. That JKD schools continue to fail or limp along in debt while their proprietors complain about successful schools is shameful. The reason is often that the instructors are horrible business people, below average teachers with horrifically confusing curriculums leading nowhere, and masters of whining.

If Original instructors really want to emulate JKD's founder they would do well to study his marketing genius. He came to America with nothing and in a few short years was giving private lessons to Hollywood elite like James Coburn and Steve McQueen and charging over $200 an hour in a time when the average yearly income in America was around $9,000. In today's numbers that would be like an instructor charging $1200 for a single private class.

These are some of the hopeless contradictions of vainly, blindly worshipping the man rather than understanding the principles that led him to such great success.

As for our view, we think that since JKD is a Wing Chun off-shoot it's instructors should be qualified to teach Wing Chun—preferably Ip Man or Wong Shun Leung Wing Chun (WSLVT) since that is exactly where Lee started his journey and would have finished had fate not intervened. Also, they should be instructed in the Driscoll/

Dempsey straight left school of boxing that so very well compliments Ip Man and WSLVT. It's that simple. The truth usually is. To do otherwise, as you've seen, brings up a multitude of trouble.

Also, as noted in the introduction, Lee didn't just add things willy-nilly. Muhammed Ali was at the peak of the boxing when Lee was putting together his JKD thoughts but the boxing that he was influenced by wasn't exactly contemporary and new. Lee actually went back to the masters of old—especially the man known as Peerless Jim Driscoll who was arguably one of the greatest pound-for-pound boxers in history. Driscoll's book, *The Straight Left and How to Cultivate It* was, according to Ted Wong, the uniting centerpiece of the new fighting method. To read it is to see clearly how Driscoll's "stop policy" became Lee's "way of the intercepting fist." Lee didn't have to look and stretch for the fencing connection because the great British boxer gave it to him in that seminal book. Thus, let us say that Lee's particular genius was not that he knew things about martial arts that no one else knew. Far from it…Lee and his method were the product of reading things others passed over and, of course, lots of hard, smart, consistent training.

Some of this gets lost both because Lee himself was so philosophical and artistic. To watch his interview with Pierre Burton—the so-called *Lost Interview*—is to see this on full display. Lee, JKD's deadly, dancing master, was as quick and nimble intellectually as he was physically. Poor Mr. Burton actually looks at the camera at one point, confusion breaking out across his face, and seems to wonder where the heck this guy came from. Lee speaks of martial arts, fighting, art, and philosophy—all while answering a single question. His fighting method wasn't something inscrutable and new but that wasn't always easy to discern when listening to him speak because he was so passionate, philosophical, and artistic all at once.

His consistent refrain to "honestly express yourself" is too often misconstrued by our narcissistic culture today as a license to do whatever they feel like doing without any reference to truth and structure. Lee, naturally, meant this quite differently—as a matter of a man having made his discipline into his own. He spoke this often as an artist, and non-artists would have no true reference point from which to comprehend his larger idea. It's good to reflect upon the fact that as a director, screenwriter, and actor, Lee brought to the world an expression of martial arts on film that simply didn't exist before him. It's easy to miss this these days when all of us have seen the transcendent and violent beauty of movies like *The Matrix*, but it was Lee that made combat visually resplendent and spiritually satisfying. When Neo and Trinity shoot up the place to free their teacher—black leather, bullets and great bodies seemingly float through time and space—the carnage isn't revolting but actually beautiful in its way. And when Bruce Lee defeats Chuck Norris in the Coliseum in their fateful battle, one witnesses two great warriors in a struggle with a deeper moral core beyond just a mere fight. There is an undeniable majesty to the action and the viewer is never cheapened by the combat or its outcome. Lee the artist showed violence in a way that made the viewer say in his soul, "wow…how great these men are" and not, "look at the blood."

It was his vision as an artist that revolutionized an entire industry and we're still benefiting from that to this very day. And his skill as an actor is quite under-appreciated too. Anyone trying to copy him has looked silly, even pathetic, because he was truly an individual—a one of a kind personality. His drama of movement and ability to convey emotion without words wasn't simply an accident. No, his electric screen presence was the result of many, many years of working on his craft and seeking improvement.

With all this said, it should be a little more clear as to why some of Lee's own statements can appear to be all over the place. He was speaking from different viewpoints frequently: the artist, the philosopher, the martial artist, and the athlete. To lose this distinction is like missing the difference between fiction and non-fiction. Of course, in our self-absorbed times, this is precisely what's happened in many respects.

Thus, we shouldn't be confused about what JKD is. It is this: Wing Chun based with oldschool boxing and not everything else. If it is everything, then it is also nothing. But the study of these combatively true principles are exactly what will free us to "express ourselves honestly in combat" because it's about principles and concepts and structures…it's not about some well connected Sifu with the perfect lineage. Jeet Kune Do and Wing Chun are not someone else's art; they don't belong to Bruce Lee or Ip Man. They belong to the focused and true practitioner who endeavors to understand the principles, practice them until they have to think about them to do them wrong, and who ultimately makes them his/her slave. This process, however, is virtually impossible in an environment where Bruce Lee is treated as some sort of god rather than a dedicated, hard-working, thoughtful man. To say that JKD is just a concept without defining that concept destroys the real process by turning the art into hyper-subjectivity. To make it out to be Bruce Lee's own personal expression begs the question of where he learned to express himself. But to know that JKD originated with Wing Chun and Peerless Jim Driscoll is to draw intimately close to the source ideas and training that inspired, taught and made Lee. Not only that, with a clear and focused understanding we can use those ideas for ourselves—thereby escaping his long, long shadow. Perhaps we shall see some even surpassing him then too.

But what of individuality? What about my god-given right to do whatever I feel like doing? Well, my modern day Protagoras disciple, who are the measure of all things, we are indeed free to follow our whims. On this we agree. What you should consider though, is that no one is free of the consequences of their actions. Reality and truth always have the last laugh on man. If you regard "doing your own thing" as the summation of mastering your craft then we have no quarrel. If you believe vainly with the modern progressives in the West that man can be "beyond system" and free of the consequences of logic, then remember other great utopian vanities. Remember the unsinkable ship (Titanic), the war to end all wars (First World War), the war on poverty (which ended poverty, right?) and so much more hubris. In truth, though an uncomfortable one, we are products of our disciplines. Our uniqueness is to be expressed through these disciplines.

An instructive point in case in Muhammed Ali. There has never been any debate within boxing circles over whether or not the great Mr. Ali was actually a boxer despite his virtually endless stylistic oddities. You see, he held his hands low (arrggghh!) bounced up and down when he moved rather than step-and-slide, never threw body shots, backed straight up, and pulled his head back instead of slipping. Yet, despite all this, Ali moved well, had blinding speed and, much needed when accompanied by the aforementioned defects—possessed a rock solid chin. You see, Ali's style was what made him unique; his method was boxing. He had mastered his discipline and made it work for him.

Many JKD/WC advocates will lose sleep, neglect pets and personal hygiene arguing over whether or not a certain Sifu is actually doing the authentic thing. Bruce Lee's primary complaint, which he learned from

Wong Shun Leung was exactly this: people focusing so much on technical particulars that they lose sight of the application universals. JKD, like it's mother art Wing Chun, and like boxing too, is a set of principles that have to be learned, trained, integrated and then, finally, applied.

THE PRACTICAL SIDE OF THINGS

Lee intended JKD to be a practical art but also one guided by true ideas (correct theory). He was a tireless proponent of truth in martial arts and had a great disdain for methods that had become too bloated and unrealistic, calling them a "classical mess". A martial art, in order to be worth studying, must work under the stress of real combat. All other benefits, like improved fitness, concentration, etc., were secondary to this basic premise. After all, who cares how good their cardio is when they're getting beaten to death because their martial art didn't work the way it was advertised? Imagine someone's dying words—after being beaten mercilessly in a fight (and having it filmed, no doubt, by inveterate losers with smart-phones)—as, "...at least I had abs of steel from P90x."

So, Lee's JKD was about real fighting (self-defense). He didn't see it as a sport since sport fighting included rules that restricted the use of tactics that the martial artist might very well need in a real fight against a foe that he wasn't matched up well against (as is the case in sport competition). Reflexes are fickle things, after all, and years of training to follow certain rules cannot be easily turned off on a moment's notice. Most methods today, being too sport-based, have no defense against basic JKD tactics like eye jabs and groin kicks as these are strictly prohibited in most methodologies. But if keeping myself as safe as possible is the goal, then the JKD fighter must be able to attack and defend the body's weakest points.

This should form the very center of all discussion on Lee's method and fighting in general. Lee unequivocally thought that a valid fighting system absolutely had to incorporate "foul" tactics and that eschewing them was a tremendous error, bordering on a kind of martial insanity. Therefore, the attack and defense of the body's weakest points must be seriously integrated into one's self-defense method if it can be considered reliable. Much controversy over what JKD is and isn't can easily be put to rest when we remember this simple point. Much complexity arises in systems that disallow or ignore foul tactics. Another way to state this is to say complexity can only thrive in an artificial environment that restricts foul tactics. Thus, JKD schools that embrace methodologies like Muay Thai, BJJ, and other MMA hybrids (to the point where they abandon JKD/Wing Chun fundamentals) are violating Bruce Lee's most central concern of fighting.

As we'll see, a great—and simple!—defense against a lot of roundhouse type punches and kicks is a counter-attack kick to the groin. Methods that prohibit this simple technique invariably complicate a fighter's defense, which causes him to lengthen his training time and engage in more dangerous and less effective methods. Moreover, by leaving such tactics out of one's system, a fighter must be a better athlete than his foe—that is, stronger and faster—because the foul tactics are, for all intents and purposes, the great equalizer between combatants.

So, in developing JKD, it's clear that Lee himself rejected methods that violated this first and critical principle. A valid system is an integration of true principles, tactics and techniques. It must be internally and externally consistent, which is another way of saying that it cannot contradict itself or the nature of fighting. Being a philosopher and avid reader, Lee was a very organized thinker in many respects, and this afforded him the ability to avoid the egregious contradictions that beset many other methods.

He recognized accurately that a physical assault was something that Boyd called a "time-crisis" and there was, therefore, no chance to do complex things. An opponent trying to rip your head off wasn't going to stand still and let you do some sort of fancy move. Lee was only interested in a system that was up to such a task.

The result of his efforts—what he called "the way of the intercepting fist"— is a masterpiece of martial thinking...brutally simple and scientifically coordinated on correct philosophical principles. It isn't "the best of a bunch of systems" as some have claimed but a unique mix of Wing Chun and old-school (British school) boxing. You might even say that Lee's JKD is a unique tactical expression of Wing Chun principles. Whatever we say on this point, we know that it's in this area that the truth is and not in the field of the myriad of other arts being taught under the banner of Jeet Kune Do. JKD is a Wing Chun/boxing vehicle—a straight hitting, highly mobile, soft-target seeking, counter-attacking method. Any attempt to fit it into another mold should be rejected unless the new approach can supersede Lee's method on these points.

DEFENSIVE BOXING, SIMPLICITY AND THE "HUNTING" FIST

As already mentioned, Bruce Lee did not just adapt boxing out of hand, but a particular type of boxing. Two of Lee's favorite boxing books were Driscoll's *Straight Left* and Jack Dempsey's *Championship Fighting: The Art of Aggressive Defense*. A little time contemplating the two titles will invariably yield great results for the careful thinker in that they encapsulate much of the soul of JKD.

You see, both Driscoll and Dempsey bemoaned the death of proper boxing in their respective books. Driscoll is especially forceful in condemning what he called the "American" brand of boxing with its over-emphasis on offense, wild swinging and poor fundamentals. Unlike Dana White today (of UFC fame), constantly exhorting his charges to "never leave it in the hands of the judges", Driscoll saw boxing as a matter of logical defense. The master of the straight lead, he writes, will only be bettered by a fighter who has superior mastery of it himself. It's easy enough to sidestep roundhouse swings—something he calls "bear-cat" brawling. A master pugilist is able to counter punch fiercely, control the distance with superb footwork and dominate with that beautiful jab. He should be so adept, Driscoll tells us, that when he retires from the fight game he should be able to do most anything else because he will still have all of his faculties.

Dempsey, on the other hand, is no stranger to defense either—despite his reputation as boxing's most dominant knockout puncher. In his book he spends ample time discussing the necessity for proper punching technique (vertical fist is a must!) and the straight lead, which he calls the "left jolt". It's rather startling to see the great Dempsey spend so much time on such a seemingly simple blow as the jab/jolt. One would expect this of Driscoll since his reputation as a defensive boxer is well known. But Dempsey explains that the leading left—combined with footwork and proper feinting, basically is boxing!

The crowd loves the knockout but it's the simple jab that paves the way for greatness.

Mike Tyson at his best was always the better jabber in the ring. In his first title bout with Trevor Berbick, it was Berbick's plan to out-jab the shorter man and push him back with the straight left—effectively cooling Tyson's explosive offense. But early Tyson was a defensive wizard and he used head-movement and footwork to score his own jab—one of which scored so solidly in the first round that Berbick abandoned his plan right then and there. Having established that brutal, machine-gun jab, Tyson dominated and dispatched Mr. Berbick in the very next round to become the Heavyweight Champion of the World. Fans remember the famous knockout. Berbick actually went down several times from a single short punch that no one saw until the replay, but it was that stiff jab in round one that really settled matters.

And it's this that Bruce Lee understood about boxing. It's the sweet science; make him miss and make him pay; simple, swift, smooth and smart. It's not about trading shots, eating punches, and mumbling your words in your later years. That boxing is really the brawling that Driscoll and Dempsey despised. Dempsey's attack was so furious—and scientific—exactly because he knew how dangerous fighting was! Dempsey wanted to get his guy out of there as quickly and safely as he could. Why take unnecessary shots?

This isn't the garden variety opinion in fighting circles. Dana White appears to like defensive fighters as much as Southerners like General

Sherman. Roy Jones Jr. was booed despite going years without losing a single round of boxing—in world title fights no less. The great Pernell Whitaker fought in front of less people than were at local Toughman contests. And Gene Tunney—who defeated Jack Dempsey twice (and Harry Greb three times!) was so unappreciated that even Will Rogers didn't care for him. The bias against great defensive fighters is so bad, so thorough, that the only ones that become famous do so mostly because they're infamous and hated. This is true of both Jack Johnson, the first black Heavyweight Champion, and Ali.

Johnson was a stellar defensive fighter—virtually untouchable. He parried and moved and clinched and punched with superlative skill. But, of course, he was utterly despised by the white community, and after some of his victories white America erupted with violence, rioting and lynchings. He didn't help himself much, by the way. He taunted his helpless white opponents. He dated and married white women and winked at them at ringside. In one case, when he was pulled over for speeding, he gave the irritated, white officer double the fine. "This is too much," the officer said. Smiling that classic, golden smile, Jack replied, "Keep it. I'm coming back this way too." This he did decades before the civil rights movement.

So, to say that he was hated is quite truly a colossal understatement. And it's exactly because he was so controversial that he's remembered, rather than for his brilliant defensive skills. Jack Johnson never proved to the paying public how tough he was for the sake of it; his boxing skills were too good and this was just another reason to hate him.

Muhammad Ali, on the other hand, is now beloved by America, but this certainly wasn't the case early in his career. His defensive skills, footwork, jab, and speed befuddled everyone he fought in the 60's. Whereas Johnson used parrying as his primary defensive tactic, Ali used his constant motion—his seemingly inexhaustible supply of energy—to deftly outmaneuver his foes. They just couldn't catch him. And this wasn't all...Ali kept telling you this too! He recited little poems he'd made up, mocking his foes and irritating his critics. When he converted to Islam, changed his name from Cassius Clay to Muhammed Ali, AND spoke out against racism, he couldn't possibly have been more despised than if he'd been in the grassy knoll in Dallas too. When he refused to be drafted he was stripped of his title and forced into three long years of exile—arguably his prime physical years.

What softened America's stance on Ali, besides his genuineness and humor, was that after his exile he engaged in those great fights with Frazier, Foreman and Norton. He did this absent of those almost preternatural reflexes of his youth. In the 70's Ali was no longer the dancing master that couldn't be touched. There was the knockdown in the 15th against Frazier, the broken jaw he fought with for 10 rounds against Norton, and the rope-a-dope against that killer, Foreman. Yes, yes...Ali won hearts with his heart. The rope-a-dope—taking a man's best shots until he tired—fans could admire. Stick-and-move perplexed them, irritated them and seemed somehow unfair. In that, I suppose, we are brethren with those savages that called for blood in the Coliseum. Blood and brokenness we can tolerate and crown with adulation; boredom and frustration we will despise. Cut off your ear! Throw down your life! Don't use your jab! How then can I be entertained?

The issue at hand is serious and extraordinarily pertinent to the JKD practitioner. On the one hand, should I smuggle into my JKD these biases against good defensive boxing and operate from the contemporary mindset that the jab is merely a set-up blow that lacks any real power, I would have abandoned the very foundation of the art. JKD is about self-defense and boxing. Truly, simply, the old, straight-hitting school is the sweet science of self-defense. Boxing grew into a sport for a variety of reasons, and as it did so it grew more viewer friendly. But I don't want my life to be a reality show and I don't want my self-defense to be an exciting spectacle—I just want it to work. If it's really exciting to watch for the average inebriated blowhard methinks that I'm taking too many shots.

Boxing as a self-defense method is virtually unheard of today—It's merely thought of as a sport but this wasn't always the case. There were schools of self-defense 200 years ago in England and in early America where boxing was taught along with the sword and cane. Today there are books around purporting to teach something called "dirty boxing" by which we are to assume that this is something new and novel. In every boxing match, though, there is a guy in a bow-tie that tells you how to box dirty. "No low blows," he says. "No holding and hitting...and no rabbit punches."

That these tactics are not allowed is precisely because they're so effective. Wing Chun students will likely note that all of these are inside tactics.

This leads us to the most serious issue with regard to defensive boxing and the public's dislike of it: it muddles the line between sport and street fighting. Our boxing forefathers knew all too well the danger of taking a bare knuckle jab to face. The introduction of gloves allowed fighters to move forward more aggressively without having to worry about every little blow. With a gloved and padded fist reckless and aggressive men were spared the true weight of their folly. A solid jab to the face—bone on bone— would cause catastrophic damage... swelling, cutting and breaking. And this is not to mention the effect of a wayward finger in the eye! Yes, the introduction of the boxing glove gave advantages to the more aggressive, less skillful boxer because it muted the ill effects of impatience. In naming his method "the way of the intercepting fist" it's clear that Bruce Lee wasn't confused on this simple point and knew well the damage a well timed counter lead could cause.

Ego and pretense not only cause people to eschew smart defensive boxing, it also causes them to pile on more technique rather than less. To use a violent but disciplined lead with precise footwork seems boring to many martial artists. They want more. They don't want simplicity of result— they want to look cool and wow people with the tons of techniques they know. But a good boxer uses his tools sparingly—applying fighting's Miranda warning that anything you throw can and will be used against you. Bruce Lee once said that JKD was simply to simplify. When we take a close look at the modifications made to his method by some students after his death, we'll see more and more complexity rather than less. And that is just the thing: any follower of Bruce Lee who doesn't seek ever more simplicity (without over simplifying, which is to say, leaving out relevant detail) has wandered off the reservation.

The summation of this point, that people don't like good defensive fighters, doesn't mean that such a style is obsolete. And what's more, the Jim Driscoll and Gene Tunney style of boxing still works despite the protestations to the contrary. Such naysayers simply don't want the style to work because they hate good boxers that use smart movement rather than pain tolerance as their primary defensive tool. If footwork, jabbing, and defensive counter-punching were obsolete how then do we explain Ali, Holmes, Leonard, Jones, and Mayweather? (And we shouldn't forget that vintage Mike Tyson, before his wretched downfall and abasement, was perhaps the best defensive heavyweight of all time). All I've done, of course, is rattle off a short list of some of the greatest boxers in history.

This, I believe, is exactly what Bruce Lee understood about boxing's unique contribution to self-defense. Seeking simple and tested things and without the defensive boxing bias that infects so many, he couldn't help but be drawn to old-school boxing. But those that are afflicted with what Richard Ryan called the "Super Man Syndrome" eschew the simple stuff that works and instead embrace various methodologies that emphasize "toughness" and/or complexity.

We should also understand that the very term "Jeet" does not mean only to stop-hit. This has been a stumbling block for many interpreters of Lee's method. I've actually heard it said, in defense of using a more complex Concepts approach to JKD, that Lee's method was about stop-hitting, which requires great speed and timing. And, they go on, since Lee was super, super fast and you're not, you can't possibly hope to stay back and play the stop-hit game. We'll ignore the fact that this logic basically says that doing something simple won't work so we should do something more complex (and one wonders how if I'm too slow to use one motion in defense, I'm fast enough to use three or four). The real problem is in the very limited interpretation of the term "Jeet".

To intercept is not, repeat not!, to sit back and wait to be attacked. The word—Jeet—can also imply hunting and stalking. We should think of a big cat in the wild— hunting. It waits for its prey to be weak, to make a mistake, and then it pounces. It doesn't sit back with its mouth open and hope the victim decides to be a meal. This misapprehension of JKD's intercepting method is widespread and most deplorable since it comes from individuals that seem to be able to conceptualize certain things but not others.

Driscoll points out in his book that there are many advantages to counter-attack over attack. First and foremost is the near certainty of the opening. There's always something open! And the counter-attacker gets to borrow force from the attacker who is moving into the strike and, further to his detriment, is limiting his own reaction time as well. Also, the counter-attacker can be reasonably certain that he will not run into a strike while firing, which is what his opponent is doing. The trick is to avoid attacking a set opponent and this is exactly why countering, i.e., intercepting is such a good idea.

When combined with the idea of stalking/hunting, the JKD fighter begins to get a more full and vigorous understanding of how countering should be applied. All manner of feints, footwork, draws, and deception factor into the game. Attack when they aren't ready—that's the key! Attack strongly into a weak position rather than a strong one. Countering/intercepting is a good way to do this. A good defensive fighter is not "fighting defensively", which is to say without aggression or determination to win. He's keeping himself from reckless exchanges through knowledge of positioning and understanding of his opponent. In this light it's all "intercepting"—even if it means launching a brutal leg kick at your opponent if he's temporarily off balance. That's still part of the intercepting/stalking/hunting framework and an expression of it.

This is the essence of JKD (and proper Wing Chun and boxing too, by the way). The techniques used in the system are physical expressions of this foundational tactical goal. When this basic premise is ignored—whether because of philosophical bias, disdain for defensive fighting, or want of complexity—there is no hope for doing JKD.

Incidentally, though I've focused mainly on the boxing side of things in this section, the same can be said for Wing Chun too. Many prominent schools preach and teach a hyper aggressive form of the system that basically says "chain punch everything until it dies!" In this they ignore counter-attacking, angle footwork, and, most importantly, bridging. In a popular reality show a few years ago, two gentleman went around the world trying out different martial arts. One of them came across a WC school in Hong Kong that prepared him for a rooftop fight with another WC student. (Since I'm not prone to walk around on rooftops I suppose I don't need to learn this style of WC.) If you've seen the episode, the reality star almost knocked out his rabidly aggressive opponent— who was trying to chain punch like it could put out a fire—but was told he lost the match because he didn't use "recognizable" WC.

Well!

Apparently, it hasn't occurred to these gentleman that they're practicing something that, when recognizable, doesn't work.

We'll happily deal with this in another volume, but it needs to be said that in Sil Lim Tao there are other techniques and ideas than chain punching. To start, when the form opens and the student crosses his hands low, then high, he's doing two things—defining the centerline and the concept of facing. Facing tells the student that he's in his best offensive position when facing. But so is the opponent if he's facing too. Duh! A little thought leads the student to understand that if they're attacking a non-facing opponent while locked in they'll have a rather formidable advantage. An anti-theoretical approach, however, will lead the student to mistakenly believe that chain punching is some kind of panacea—a redoubtable technique from which there's no escape.

RECENT TRENDS AND JKD

We must remember that Lee sought a self-defense method and not a fighting sport. Roundhouse blows which leave the middle of the body vulnerable to attack were not to be emphasized and, just as well, the center of the body—housing weak targets like nose, eyes, throat, and groin—were absolutely to be attacked. And good footwork was much to be emphasized since it simplified defense. A sidestep is better than a block, after all and a moving target is harder to hit than a stationary one. Once more, roundhouse blows fall out of favor with JKD theory in that they also impede free movement (footwork) and are more disruptive to one's balance than straighter blows. As a consequence, if one seeks a system where they can move at a maximum, hit weak targets, and stay as small a target as possible while doing so, they must endeavor to hit straight.

Another way to see this is the opposite. Imagine a system where we strike only at the foe's strongest points, move as little as possible, fire every strike so that it robs our balance and leaves us exposed. That's not a system of self-defense, it's a system of self-abuse. You would have to be markedly better conditioned than your foe to prevail (not to mention that you'll have to hope he doesn't get lucky and pop you in the groin). You couldn't get a system more opposed to what Lee was doing and yet this is exactly what passes as JKD in some circles.

All of this confusion stems from ignoring the obvious facts of Bruce Lee, Wing Chun, boxing, and his philosophy. However, if we aim to keep the main thing the main thing, we'll do well. Talk of soft-targets and the like are relevant within the realm of self-defense, which is something that many arts—especially here in the West—are not any more; they are systems of sport. Lee's interest in boxing, for example, wasn't because he wanted to compete or thought that his students should either. No, it was because boxing—like wrestling—had achieved a certain level of simple effectiveness because its' training always required limited and defined non-cooperation between students. This created aliveness and limited the accumulation of unrealistic techniques and tactics.

There is a trade-off, of course. Methods that compete against each other like boxing, wrestling, Muay Thai, MMA, etc., have to have some kind of safety rules in order for there not to be bloodshed. Lee understood this quite necessary transaction and was smart to see that many martial arts didn't have terrible technique ideas so much as they had unrealistic training habits. A boxer who is used to his opponent moving and hitting back is better prepared for real combat than a karate student who is used to his training partner throwing a punch and leaving his arm extended, waiting for the inevitable beat-down. The hard part is finding the right balance between functional training practices and real-life techniques so that the student has both aliveness and proper defensive tools to use.

Sport-based systems have a tendency to avoid the "complexity creep" that chokes other systems simply because the rigors of competition allow truly meritorious techniques a showcase. More than just that, though—because you have an opponent (within the sports' rules) doing their best to defeat and frustrate your technique, unproductive methods will result in your harm. Competition, therefore, because it provides ruthless accountability, provides a kind of refiners fire that stands sentinel against the encroachment of useless baggage and bad ideas.

Complexity creep (or arm-chair rule, whatever you want to call it) is forever before us, tempting us to abandon the tried and true. This is especially evident in the field of government, where employees (bureaucrats) are very often sheltered from the results of their ideas—not to mention that they use other people's money instead of their own. A soldier with bad ideas ends up a dead soldier. A fireman with unrealistic ideas on how to fight a fire ends up a crispy critter at worst, or with a gutted building in the least. This is generally why the average layperson respects the soldier, fireman, and police officer but naturally regards the politician with suspicion. The former have their ideas tested and if they find them wanting, they are the first to suffer.

A quick quiz: where would you rather go—to the DMV to renew your license or to the internet to shop/browse? Obviously, no one goes to the DMV unless they absolutely have to—and because people only go when they have to, the DMV has limited incentive to improve its performance. At the DMV there is no pain for them if their customer service is poor whereas in private business there is. On the internet everyone is competing for your attention and business. Thus, there is risk of loss (pain) if unproductive habits and practices dominate. The internet is the last and best free market left today. It has spurred tremendous growth, innovation, and wealth exactly because it has been free—and freedom means testing! It's human nature—in the kwoon, dojo, business, or government—to try and stack the deck so that we don't have to risk failure anymore. Consequently, the consolidation of power—whether by a so-called master/ sensei/sifu, boss, or bureaucrat—is always a dangerous, regrettable thing. The concept of reality testing applies to all of life, and wherever we see people, groups or governments rejecting it we know that stagnation, mediocrity, and maybe even tyranny are close behind. It can be called many things: seniority, tenure, contract-guarantee...whatever name it goes by it is all the same—I want to shelter myself from the consequences of my conduct...I don't want failure to be an option anymore. This being so, a free and intelligent people should always resist institutions, governments and personal practices that reject accountability through realistic testing.

Testing, in whatever means it may come, keeps us from becoming complacent and shot-through with delusions of our skill and worth. Lee's goal to "hack away the unessential" could only be met by the truth-seeking that embraces accountability.

Consequently, Bruce Lee saw sparring as essential to JKD because it offered a relatively safe view of actual skill. Better to find out in sparring if you can't block a punch or stuff a takedown attempt than in a real fight, right? Who cares if your teacher could do it or if the system is good. Can *you* do it? That is what Lee was getting at, and any system that purports to do something must be able to produce results. Many classical arts of Lee's time had completely eschewed any type of testing. Their katas were hopelessly long and seriously divorced from reality. He rightfully scoffed at this the same way a surgeon would at a witch doctor. So, in the 60's, long before MMA had ever taken its first baby step, Lee was donning gloves and gear and going out to spar.

Indubitably, this ushered in a brave new world of realism in the martial arts.

Unfortunately, as we've seen, not all of this has been good. Embracing the sport-based testing ideas of JKD, modern martial arts has been enraptured by the bright lights of cage fighting and the UFC. Yes, it's more realistic than learning to break boards that don't hit back, but that doesn't make it real. It's like the military engaging in an actual war with war-game rules in place. Plus, all live testing (sparring and chi-sao for our purposes) can be dangerous, and since they are means to an end, safety should be of the utmost concern. MMA offers much by way of realistic means-testing but is far more dangerous to its participants while also forcing them to eschew simpler tactics (groin, throat, eye attacks, etc.) in favor of more complex ones. If your goal is to be an MMA fighter then you absolutely need to do MMA, but using their tactics of training for JKD is, well, dangerous and wrongheaded.

Sparring is vastly more dangerous than supervised boxing, where 16oz. gloves, etc., are required and the sparring partners are training with the right goals in mind and not, repeat not, abusing one another for the heck of it. Sure, it's tough; you can get banged around but you shouldn't get beaten up. MMA uses gloves that are too small to adequately protect their fighters from cuts and hand injuries. Their regular training techniques also include kicks, knees, elbows, and take-downs. All of these weapons in play make it very easy for accidents to happen in training. I know of several fighters that have suffered the loss of teeth (from ducking into a knee strike), have blown out their ACLs (from a takedown attempt), and have broken bones from submissions that went too far. All of these are severely life altering injuries that have happened during MMA training.

MMA sparring is wrongheaded for the JKD student too because it trains the ground fighter to use complex moves where simple ones would be best. For real scenarios, ground fighting and clinch work must include foul tactics—eye gouge, groin hits, etc. These skills must be trained often enough to be automated. However, due to restrictions in MMA about hitting soft targets, those who train in MMA will not be drilling these "dirty" tactics into their fighting subconscious. Eschewing your primary targets while defending against a neck-tie or take-down will demand that you train more complex moves rather than simple ones. Therefore, when under pressure, your reflex will be more to pull guard, for example, than to eye gouge or throat grab your attacker. Additionally, your own defense against such "dirty" tactics will be diminished because you are not actively considering them in everyday training.

An old friend of mine was fond of saying "balance is key" and I do believe that there is much wisdom in that approach. We are always prone to swing to one extreme or the other and, in the process, leave out critically relevant details. This was a mistake that Lee didn't make because he astutely recognized and clung to the basic truths he'd discovered. The theologian/philosopher Norman Geisler says that in reference to the truth one should, "get all they can, can what they get, and sit on the lid." This is precisely what Lee did and it was the source of his brilliance; he kept the main thing the main thing.

Using sport type drills like sparring (with varying levels of intensity) is a great way to enhance a student's skill level and we do well in JKD when we continue to look for new and updated ways to challenge ourselves in training. But adapting MMA wholesale is another thing altogether and confuses a training aid for the real thing. With this said, if you're taking JKD someplace and aren't doing any "open" drills like boxing and chi-sao, where your partner gets to move and hit back, you are likely in the wrong place. Fighting is all about reaction. If all you do is stand around trapping or working on "perfect" technique and no one ever really tries to hit you, you will never have any idea if the skills you've learned are ever truly real-world ready. Instructors of this kind of method generally spend a lot of time bad-mouthing those uncouth barbarians who get in and "mix it up", but when you think about it, you've never actually seen Super-Sifu in environments where their rival can freely attack. As Lee was fond of saying, anyone can appear to be a master when he dictates the circumstances. My advice: run from these egomaniacal charlatans. Your skill and character depend on it. As for the claim that your JKD/Wing Chun is for "the real world" and you don't wear "pillows" on your hands, have rules, and other such bombast, we should remember that sparring is a drill. It's a part of training—not a fight itself. Imagine a soldier who never practices defensive drills—he just shoots at the range—because he says that in "real war" he'd be firing to really kill someone. But we know that soldiers and police practice things like entering buildings, clearing rooms, etc. It's not the real thing…it's part of the drill process in order to automate good habits needed under stress. Sparring is like this.

Even if Super-Sifu is sure that his skills don't require any live, unscripted testing like contact sparring, what about his students? My thought is to let my students go out there and see for themselves—but as safely as possible and with supervision. Many, many myths evaporite when the opponent is moving and firing back. And all this nonsense about MMA guys and boxers being limited by rules becomes moot because they have experience scoring and taking shots and you don't. Of course, sparring isn't fighting, nor should it be, but the rantings of people who clamor on about so called real fighting but never engage in sparring seems like special-pleading. They do forms; they do drills. Sparring is simply an extension of that.

Another area of confusion for JKD today comes from the emergence of the so-called Reality Martial Arts (RMA). This development is, one would assume, somewhat in response to the ever worsening violent crime within our increasingly amoral culture and the ubiquitous nature of sport-based systems. But RMA has also flourished, I believe, because of the misconceptions that have grown since Lee's untimely death in 1973. Either way, RMA has developed quite a niche in the martial arts market. Methods like Krav Maga are sold to the public as being realistic when, in fact, they are actually a body without a head. The central issue is in the mis-identification of reality (eschewing a simpler answer) and poor training habits. In truth, RMA is functionally worse than traditional systems in dealing with the real world.

First, it spends the vast majority of its training time dealing with the defeat of an armed assailant. But the best defense against a knife or gun is another weapon, not a disarm (which, by the way, precious few people have ever actually pulled off). I have a knife and gun for precisely this problem. Don't bring a side-kick and pak-da to a gun fight! One has to wonder why it's a good idea to spend 90% of your training time preparing for an absolute worse case scenario that pleads for other options.

Just as bad, the disarms of knives and guns are always practiced against a stationary, compliant partner. In this, RMA is really Aikido without the gi, break-falls and, well, the rest of the system. But one small change in the dynamic of the confrontation renders the vast majority of disarms unusable for the very reason that the defender has to be absolutely perfect and the armed assailant merely needs to be mediocre (on a scale of application). These are daunting odds when your life is on the line, we should note. What works well in the school—where the gun holder is still and, most importantly, within arms reach—might very well get you killed when the gun holder is too far away and waving the gun about nervously.

So, on the one side of JKD we have the proliferation of sports-based systems and on the other side the RMA movement. Neither is as beneficial for real self-defense as is JKD because neither has the correct balance of theory and practice. The philosopher Gordon Clark said that "all practice is the practice of some theory." Today, especially in the anti-intellectual West, we are decidedly anti-theory, which explains these two splinters of MMA and RMA being mistaken for real world self-defense. One method forgets that the rules limitation has distorted its perception of what really works and the other forgets that there is no real aliveness (realism) in its training. On the whole, I will add though, the former is fine to exist solely as a sport (regardless of what your evaluation of MMA is as a form of entertainment) but the latter (RMA) is most over-daring in making mortals think that they can ever be masters over knives and guns with their bare hands.

Another point to consider is the "who, what, when, where and why" of fighting. In regard to RMA, why are you fighting an armed assailant in the first place and how did he get the drop on you? A decent handgun of your own might cost a few hundred dollars. If you're so concerned with facing an armed assailant you really would do well to even the odds beforehand by having your own weapon. If, on the other hand, you work/live in a high risk environment—handling large sums of cash, have a meth lab in your trailer, are cheating with a Navy Seal's wife, draw images of the Prophet Muhammad for your local paper—you probably need bodyguards, not Krav Maga. Other than that, a concealed weapon permit is the way to go. Remember: don't bring your bare hands to a gun or knife fight.

This isn't to say that Lee's JKD and Wing Chun are a middle ground between the two approaches. No, it's more than that. It's the correct relationship between combat theory and practice. It uses certain testing procedures (like sparring with protective gear and chi-sao to name the most prominent) and correct, simple principles to form a non-contradictory whole. Lee understood that there needed to be verifiable means within a system to test and develop application skill, or else his system would merely go on to be a good looking corpse. To this end, Lee incorporated some boxing style (sport-based) training but that is all it was—training. He never confused what was the means and what was the end as some of his followers have gone on to do. Moreover, as the RMA movement purports to do, Lee's JKD is meant to deal with the real world.

And, incidentally, we'll cover the use of JKD's testing exercises, like sparring and chi-sao, in another volume as that is a subject requiring its own study. But for now, let us concern ourselves with the foundation.

HONOR AND COMBAT THEORY

Before we commence our survey of basic techniques it behooves us to spend some time ascertaining the moral and tactical considerations that the physical techniques seek to address. It's a common problem, really, for martial artists to begin "mid-stream" and think only of techniques rather than philosophy and strategy. These considerations are perhaps the most neglected and misunderstood aspects in all of fighting.

Many times I've had a new student start at our Academy after years of training in another system and they've remarked that they'd never had things like strategy and tactics addressed systematically—if at all. This omission of the brain-game of fighting leaves students at the mercy of their attributes and experience. They learn from simply being in there—sparring and wrestling and whatnot. But absent of a conceptual underpinning—of correct theory—no student is ever able to reasonably apprehend the truth of combat over against their own system's means testing. This is to say that the BJJ student will learn much from constantly working against a resistant opponent in training, but if he's not given correct theory, then he is handicapped as far as applying his skills in the dynamic environment of real-world violence.

To know how, Bruce Lee pointed out often to his students, means to know when and why. Another way of seeing this is to again say that all practice is the practice of some theory. There is no human endeavor that can succeed in being liberated from theory; there is always that mind/body connection. Of course, we live in an age where even our educators boast of their systemic/philosophic ignorance. Everyone is a specialist and philosophy is dead. But we cannot afford, as martial artists, to engage in this sort of irresponsible thinking because violence and self-defense is not a rather forgiving subject. A biologist can get along with pretending that philosophy doesn't matter (this is a philosophical assertion, though). An expert in violence, on the other hand, must understand correct theory or their practice could very well end up making them dead and/or the immoral aggressor.

As we've already discussed, a fight is not a match. All-out fighting doesn't have the benefits of boxing or MMA such as sure footing, time limits, rules against foul tactics, designated start time, prohibition against weaponry and multiple opponents, and so on. These must all be considered seriously as we begin to put our fighting method together. And since real fighting tends to be unpredictable, sudden and chaotic, simplicity is an absolute key. If it's easy to do in training, it will be hard to do in a real fight; if it's hard to do in training, it's likely never to work in a real fight. Thus, the bedrock principle of JKD—one that Lee believed in mightily—was that of simplicity.

Once, under the supervision of Ted Wong, my kung-fu brother, Jonathan Parsons, and I were practicing. We were supposed to be countering the one-two. Instead, I'm thinking, "wait 'til Bruce Lee's private student sees what I can do." Rather stupidly (because I really should have known better at that point) I began to counter Jonathan's punches with an increasing array of complexity. At first: a parry and groin kick. After this seemed unimpressive to Sifu Wong, I parried the jab, slipped the cross, and countered with my own cross to the body, followed by a trap and hit and then a takedown. More is better, right? Well, this went on for a while...with Jonathan and I consistently trying to out-do one another in martial complexity. Ted Wong watched all this with what appeared to be disdain (as much as that emotion seemed possible to the ever humble and unassuming instructor).

Finally, in exasperation, I paused from our motley mix of martial mayhem and asked, "Well...Sifu...what do you think?"

I'd waited too long to be praised by Bruce Lee's personal student and could no longer stand not hearing him tell me how impressive I was. So I asked and waited humbly for the accolades to flow, describing my superlative skill, proclaiming me to be heir of all things JKD. Instead, he stood there with his arms crossed and shifted his weight, thinking. "Well," he began with a shrug, "one movement?" He gave us a thumbs up. "Two movements?" He held out his hand and made a so-so gesture. "Three movements?" He shook his head dismally. Then the killer. "You guys?" He raised his hands to his nose and didn't say that we stunk but we got the message.

Jonathan and I still laugh about that to this very day.

You will no doubt be shocked at how little you see by way of technique here and that is by deliberate, painful design. Simplicity must absolutely be the central principle around which our techniques and tactics revolve. JKD is meant to simplify! Everywhere that we see a tremendous problem in life, seemingly implacable and mind-numbingly difficult, it is likely because we have rejected a simple truth from the outset. Old-school bare-knuckle boxing and Wing Chun both run to simplicity and are counter-attacking striking arts that rely on the straightest, most direct attack possible.

Some very key fundamentals for us to absorb:

A counter attack is the best form of defense and a straight hit is the best form of counter attack because straight hits give you the following advantages:

- Faster

- More accurate

- Less disruption of balance so you can actually both move and fire

- Higher rate of fire available

- Less chance of you injuring your hand or foot

- You're a smaller target

- Less telegraphic

- Greater power through proper structure

Also, there are only four things you should be doing in a fight. First, maintain a "fighting measure". The measure is often misunderstood as a purely sport term but it's infinitely more important than this. The measure in fighting is like proper following distance in driving. If you're too close you don't have enough time to respond to an attack. Generally in hand-to-hand fighting the measure is where your opponent has to step to you to attack. Once this distance is breached you must already be doing the other three things which we'll get to in a moment.

But first, the measure could be a situation where you have a hostile man in front of you. At a safe distance of several feet he's telling you what a jerk you are, berating you, calling you profane things, etc. Immediately look to exit the environment while also placing your hands up—palms forward—and telling him you don't want any trouble. (Apologize even if you didn't do anything wrong...don't worry about ego, just leave). As you begin to move away your agitator has a choice to either let you break away or pursue. Or, perhaps, one of his cronies decides to flank you. In either event, once your foe or potential foe begins to move into the measure and/or cut off your exit, you should counter-attack rather than wait for his attack. This is what we mean by "hit first" in our mantra of "hit first, hit straight, hit hard, hit often."

One of the most unfortunate misconceptions regarding self-defense is that you can wait for an attack to start and then begin a successful counter. But action is faster than reaction, of course, and in a violent encounter where fractions of seconds have dire consequences, waiting for your enemy to start is, in the least, a poor plan. Doing a drill like "four corner defense" in class is just that—a drill. Just because you've been taking classes in the world's coolest martial art doesn't mean you are contractually obligated to try every thing you do in class. If at all possible, attack and/or run the very moment before the critical gap of space (fighting measure) closes.

At this point good people are often at a significant disadvantage because, being peaceable and civilized, they don't want to harm others. Modern Western society, in fact, has made us especially vulnerable to predators in that we live lives of extraordinary comfort and ease and are shot through with delusions of safety. It is absolutely essential, therefore, for a martial artist to cultivate a healthy sense of fear (not to be confused with paranoia) and realize when action is necessary and hesitation is deadly.

Fighting defensively, that is to say, waiting for the attack and then responding, is a horrible tactic. Note in Bruce Lee's JKD lesson on Longstreet he is ready for the attack when he instructs his inquirer to attack. "Come on...touch me..." But he's set already! Our interception policy has to be proactive. Bad guys send signals; they target and set-up their prey. There are two things needed for a sucker punch to land: a punch and a sucker. A sucker is anyone who leaves himself in a potentially violent place where the aggressor can get a drop on them. Real fights are seldom, if ever, fair.

Just a quick glance at military history will emphasize this point. It was clear to everyone with a brain in 1941 that Hitler was planning an attack on the Soviet Union. Nazi forces were massing all along the border in alarming numbers and yet Stalin couldn't bring himself to believe that invasion was imminent despite the clear military signs. Millions of German soldiers along with thousands of tanks and seemingly limitless artillery were precariously organizing in the spring of 1941, obviously ready to make a dash across Ukraine. Hitler and German diplomats assured the Russians that they were just there for maneuvers. "Sure, I've already attacked England, France, Poland, etc.," Hitler was saying, "but I'd never do that to you, Josef. You're my buddy. Trust me. Yes, yes...I hate communists and hunt, imprison and murder commies here in Germany but you and me—well, we're allies." In June, however, the largest invasion the world had ever seen was launched.

Stalin was in shock, inconsolable. Being out of touch with reality has a tendency to do that to you when the signs you've been ignoring suddenly turn into the event you refused to think about much less prepare for.

That Soviet Russia actually survived and prevailed should not suggest to us that sitting on your hands while your enemy loads up is forgivable. Soviet losses were so bad as to be literally unthinkable. By some estimates they lost 26 million soldiers and civilians in their war with Hitler. Yes, they crushed the famed 6th Army at Stalingrad and repelled the attack on Moscow. And, certainly, they exacted a terrible revenge on Berlin a few short years later but the price they paid for this victory was a loss so staggering that historians still marvel at it.

This and countless other examples from history show us that on average the only way to prevail when a fight starts that you were ill prepared for is to absorb an extraordinary amount of damage and then come roaring back. The problem is that our analogy breaks down at this point because we only have our own body to sacrifice if we're the sucker. Maybe we get lucky. Maybe not. Either way, the fighting measure isn't just a static sport term regulating distance. It's a powerful tactical concept directing us to do everything in our power to make sure we have the ability to withstand an enemy assault.

Parenthetically, as important as it is to avoid the "normalcy bias" as it's called (believing that something can't happen simply because it hasn't happened to you before) it's equally important to practice the art of preclusion. Preclusion, simply put, is the art of acting with an eye towards the legal ramifications of violence. If you can't reasonably prove that any other person in your situation would have been in fear for their life (or grave injury) and that escape wasn't possible, your attack will be deemed (and probably is) a criminal action.

In one instructive case—the Hockey Dad incident a few years back— two dads, Thomas Junta and Michael Costin, got into an argument over their son's game. Junta was irritated that his son was getting roughed up (hard checking and even a wayward elbow) in what was supposed to be a non-contact practice. When he complained to Costin who was supervising, Costin is said to have replied, "that's hockey." A scuffle ensued afterwards but the men were separated by other parents. At that point according to the record, Junta left but returned because his son was still inside. How the next fight started is debatable depending upon the witness. Some said Costin sucker-punched Junta. Others said that Junta went right after Costin. Either way, Costin was killed when a blood vessel burst in his neck causing severe brain damage.

In the end, a jury convicted Junta of involuntary manslaughter and a judge sentenced him to 6-10 years in prison. What mattered legally in this instance is that there were enough witnesses that claimed Junta was angry and wanted to fight. Moreover, some claimed that they screamed at him to stop hitting the fallen Costin even though Junta insisted he only landed three off-balance blows. In short, Junta's preclusion defense—an insistence that he had no other choice but to fight and that any reasonable person would have fearfully done the same thing—was shattered. Violence, unlike in the movies and video games, always carries with it consequences and emotional baggage. Violence is nasty business. Fighting is brutal, ugly, and contrary to the ways of any peace-loving person, or society. Junta went to jail—his life ruined—and another man was dead because of a hockey match between children.

How utterly tragic.

If you don't have any other choice, though, and you must make the regrettable decision to fight, the other three things you must be doing is hitting (preferably straight, though this includes pushing, pulling, and using your environment to the best of your ability), moving, and clinching. To be inside the "hot-zone" where your opponent can reach you without doing one of these three things—or a combination thereof—is to be driving with your eyes closed, only something is going to hit you instead of you hitting it. We'll have to get more into this subject in the later volume on training and tactics. The other issue that concerns us before we turn to our techniques is that of morality.

Much literature is written on violence by writers who have been trained to think of men as nothing more than advanced apes. But we are moral beings and a Skinners Box approach is lacking in that it leaves ethics and morality out of the study of life's most profoundly ethical enterprise: combat. It should be evident, therefore, that violence is not capable of ever producing value, meaning, beauty, or love. Violence can be used in protection of these things but never in their production. Violence and force are antithetical to all that is good, true, beautiful and excellent; to love violence for its own sake is to be a most hideous moral reprobate. Patrick Swayze's character, Dalton, in *Roadhouse*, that cult classic film, had a great line. He said, "no one ever wins a fight." This is as true a statement as can be uttered because it encapsulates all that we've considered here.

What savage passions are released within a culture that produces art that glorifies meaningless sex and morally-neutral violence! It's absolutely a chilling time to be alive in that ours is the very first culture to ever exist (Western democracies) that have not had an explicit moral code—having rejected Judeo-Christianity and replaced it with the shifting sands of humanism. The terrible violence that we continue to see erupt around us are but the first bellows of a mighty volcano set to erupt throughout our land. Human beings are moral beings, and right and wrong matter. To raise generations of young men and women that believe that there is no ultimate moral code is the equivalent of societal suicide.

Every martial artist everywhere should worry about the denigration of moral principles because there is a world of difference between fending off a rogue individual and withstanding the savagery of a decadent society. Thucydides said long ago that "the society that separates its scholars from its warriors will have its thinking done by cowards, and its fighting done by fools." So, indeed, martial artists should not be ignorant or indifferent on matters of morality. Those trained and schooled in the ways of violence absolutely must be the first to understand the ugliness that results from the use of force—between men or nations. To be ambivalent towards issues such as justice, mercy, peace and yet be trained to fight is to be an awful, walking dichotomy. We are called to be higher than that.

In my many years in martial arts it's been a terrible and sad fact that a good many teachers of the warrior arts are more bully than servant/leader; they are Cobra-Kai rather than Miyagi. Many of these men teach because they are strong—not because they wish to make others strong.

So, I will make no attempt to avoid the obvious as to do so imperils our collective ability to live in peace, love our families and pursue the values that make life meaningful and wonderful. A man that has been raised to believe that others owe him something is a dangerous man. All children need unconditional love and loving discipline. Absence of this, as writer Peggy Noonan has said, produces fear and resentment in our young. As our families disintegrate and more young men come of age knowing only such emotions they become enraged. They are unloved; they are wounded deeply in their soul by a culture that has devastated the family and made good fathers few and far between. This is a recipe for disaster.

So these young men yearn for acceptance and meaning. They join gangs. They do drugs. And they produce another generation more scarred and angry than they are.

Since you're reading this (and this far into it) it's safe to assume that you're a serious martial artist. If you're like me then you spend a great amount of time training. In my own case, nary a week goes by in my life that I haven't had multiple people throwing kicks and punches at me of various sorts in a variety of drills. It's a strange brotherhood. We sweat and toil; we spar and train. We talk about our performance and study the game intensely—and, yes, we laugh about our mistakes and enjoy the camaraderie. Most of my deepest friendships have developed through the martial arts. Truly I'm blessed.

So, we love the warrior arts but this isn't to say that we love violence. Warriors love honor and the defense of what is true and, in many cases, vulnerable. Savages use force to elevate themselves. A true warrior loves the discipline and skill for their own sake and for the sake of what he can defend. A bully ultimately loves only himself and truth and honor are things to be discarded when he can't get his way.

In this regard, I take special delight in the example set by Bruce Lee in his movies. In every film he takes great care to use force only when he absolutely has to—and, especially, only against those that have violated the weak.

A few years ago an adult student of mine—a married father of two young boys—had an affair and left his wife. His sons also took our classes. I found out about this tumult when his then-wife told me that she was going to have to pull the kids from the classes for a while due to financial strain. When I asked the father about it later he confessed that there was another woman. His soon to be ex-wife hadn't cheated on him first or done anything other than be the loving, doting mother of his two boys. I asked him if he thought he was a martial artist. He looked at me weirdly and replied, somewhat uneasily, "yeah...I guess so."

"No," I said sadly. "You have no code—no honor." Almost pleadingly I went on. "To those most vulnerable around you—your family—you've assaulted their sense of security, you've annihilated their trusting hearts and you've turned them to the arms of bitterness and coldness. You took a vow publicly before God and man to be faithful. Your wife built her life upon that vow and raised your children in the trust of your solemn word. But today you declare for all to see that convenience is more important to you then the lives and hearts of those that most need you. You have broken your word and the hearts of those most dependent upon you. A martial artist must have honor; you've thrown yours away for the fleeting pleasures of your flesh. A man must protect his family, yet you've violated yours in the most intimate way possible. Repent of this! Beg God's forgiveness and theirs."

He teared up—his heart obviously pierced. But he'd gone too far, apparently, down that contemptible path so he fought the better side of his nature and left.

Tragically, this isn't the only or even the worst example of our desultory ethics wreaking havoc upon our homes and hearts today. I illustrate it in the hope to remind us all that if we study and train for violence we do so only in the service of the good. And what greater mockery can we make of our efforts than to cause the damage we say we guard against? Isn't it the honor—not merely the skill—that moves us when we see Donnie Yen in Ip Man or Jet Li in Fearless? And, if we're sincere, isn't it honor that we wanted when we first started our martial journey? Honor serves love with strength and self-control. Honor dictates that we strive always to do what's right rather than what we feel like doing. Honor never demands of others what they won't freely give and what isn't earned. And people of honor keep their word!

Imagine a world full of people of this sort just described. What would we have to fear?

Our ruinous culture today mocks honor. Everywhere it's taught and proclaimed that doing what you feel like doing isn't simply something to be tolerated, but that all manner of ill-behavior is to be accepted. The true problem, society today tells us, lies not in vice but in the condemnation of vice—that's the real vice! But, alas, God is not mocked and we see all around us the calamitous consequences of years of amorality. Broken homes, corporate and government corruption built upon personal turpitude, and every day more and more mind-numbing violence. YouTube is a veritable highlight reel of societal decay. Mobs beat and rob weak people and savages cheer and film the moral insanity with their phones rather than call the police. (And, of course, they put the whole sordid thing on the internet too!)

With all of this said, it's incumbent upon us—those who practice and teach the use of force—to be vigilant, to be men and women of the utmost honor. If it cannot be said of us that we are humble, gentle, trustworthy, slow to anger, and servant-leaders, then our advanced fighting skills are to be bemoaned rather than applauded. If we are a terror to our families, trusted by no one—feared but not respected—then our skills are the embellishments of a villain and we should renounce our practice of the use of force until such time that we have learned humility and put on love. A man is no man that counts his vanquished as his achievement.

A true martial artist sees those lives he's helped build and protect, like a soldier writing home would, thinking of his land, his family and his flag as his success. If we have the fighting skills of an Achilles but sport a tattered family and failed friendships due to our own virtueless, noxious character we are deceiving ourselves. We're savage, not men of honor.

Let us not allow our great endeavor, the martial arts, to be in truth the last refuge of skilled scoundrels. Society will forever need the existence of men of arms to lead and protect exactly because there are so many who fail to heed the call for character. And, please, if these words fail to stir your heart, if they are dead to you, read no further as you have no place in the family of warriors. An honest man's battle against evil must always begin within his own heart, for there it is that the enemy resides. Should we refuse to acknowledge this and go forth under the presumption that we can do no wrong, that it's others who are always the problem, then pride—that most vile, sneaky, and hidden cancer—will eat through our souls. We must not allow this.

A life dedicated to the martial arts is one in which we have a high calling to subdue, not an external enemy, but anger, malice, deceit, greed, covetousness, envy, and lust in our own hearts. These are the vile things lurking in the hearts of men that cause violence, not poverty or whatever new ill the politicos obsess about. A life of peace is bought only with righteousness, goodness, and love and to try and attain it any other way will invariably fail. As governments tried to appease Hitler in the 1930's we should not try and appease the evil in our own lives.

We do well to remember that hand-to-hand combat cannot be a voluntary activity in a civil society. Escape (walking away, avoiding problem areas, basic prevention measures, etc.) will always be preferable to fighting. Moreover, if I am in a true self-defense situation, I should have the moral and legal right to defend myself with a weapon. For example, if an intruder attacks me in my home the only reason I would engage him hand-to-hand is because I couldn't get to my shotgun fast enough. Just as well, there are precious few scenarios in daily life where I don't have ample opportunity to run and/or put a barrier between me and my assailant. Should someone attack me in a parking lot there are virtually limitless heavy objects for me to place between me and my attacker. So, unless I've severely ticked off Bruce Banner, I doubt that my Toyota Tundra will be tossed aside if I start to run around it.

Naturally, this sounds foreign to those who think a fight is a match. But that is ego talking—not self-preservation. In most locations, incidentally, if you haven't tried to avoid the fight—if escape wasn't impossible—you cannot legally claim self-defense. Even still, just because something is legal doesn't automatically mean it's moral too. Using a weapon—whether it's our own body or a gun—should never be done flippantly, and special care must be taken to avoid any unnecessary confrontation. As it's written, "so long as it depends on you, live peaceably with all." Of course, States that disallow the use of deadly force in the defense of your home/business have pushed the limit too far in the other direction because that gives the intruder yet another advantage. Nevertheless, it's inherently moral to make sure that law supports the preservation of peace in every way it can and that it views avoidable violence as a criminal act.

This reality gives backbone and clarity to Bruce Lee's intercepting method. JKD is first and foremost a counter-attacking method—as well it should be. It's entire DNA is set up for defense (that being a vigorous counter attack, of course) rather than offense.

THE JEET KUNE DO ON-GUARD STANCE

JKD starts with the on-guard stance. This stance is a unique adaptation of the Wing Chun stance. Whereas in WC there is said to be a leg forward but no leading side, JKD favors the strong side slightly forward for distance fighting. Thus, a right-hander will place their right side forward. But the leading side should not dominate the rear—or cut it off. If the back foot is directly behind the front it will impede lateral movement and make the rear hand/foot difficult to bring into action. Thus, the rear foot should be slightly across from the lead foot's position. This position allows the JKD fighter to move freely in any direction and have access to both sides of the body for offense and defense. (In Wing Chun this stance is introduced in the 2nd form and is referred to as the Chum Kui Ma.)

The hands should be raised in a relaxed position in front of the body, elbows in and pointing to the floor. If the elbows point outward the fundamental structure of the stance is compromised as the arms are no longer connected to the rest of the body. Furthermore, elevating the elbows opens the trunk up to assault and grappling and also puts unnecessary stress on the deltoids. This can all be avoided by making sure the elbows stay "inside" the shoulders. Incidentally, continued practice of Wing Chun's Sil Lim Tao will greatly assist the JKD student in developing the proper feel for this stance.

As you can guess from the name of our art (Way of the Intercepting Fist), the straight punch is the backbone of JKD's offense and defense. The hand position of the JKD on-guard stance is designed to facilitate the economical delivery of straight punches. The hands (fists) should be held forward from the trunk and not pinned backward, against the body and/or face. To do so gives our punches more ground to cover and puts us in a more defensive position than necessary. If the arms are forward from the trunk, however, they form a good defensive barrier as well as offering an advanced launching point for counter-attacks and stop-hits. Again, borrowing from the WC system, JKD employs the "immovable elbow" principle, which is to say that the elbows don't collapse against the body, thus pinning them.

Simplicity and non-telegraphic motion are very important principles in JKD. Keeping the arms forward from the body extends your defensive perimeter considerably and is an absolute must when confronted with a bare-knuckle assailant. A historical point to consider: boxers now carry their guard against their body and face because of their gloves. The back of the hand isn't a very good defensive tool (nor are your knuckles driving into your temple from the force of a "blocked" blow). Without padded gloves a fighter is far smarter to move their hands/arms forward. This will come in very handy for parrying. Furthermore, bringing your guard forward also makes your strikes faster in that they have less ground to cover. Keeping your hand unnecessarily pinned against your chin when bare-fisted makes your punches travel nearly twice the distance to your target—thus my contention that this is a built-in telegraphic motion in that it gives the opponent more time to react. And, as it goes, you already have enough trouble, don't help your opponent out even more.

The purposes of the JKD on-guard stance are:

- Provide optimal position for delivery of primary strikes
- Provide optimal balance between mobility and stability
- Provide the best (within reason since there's always something open) defensive posture without interfering with the first two goals

It must be understood that, in fighting, all of these things (as well as those that follow) are taking place instantaneously. Therefore there is no division between these points and they must be fully integrated. This will be said again, but it bears repeating: just adding things willy-nilly and calling it JKD is a dangerous and irrational game to play in that integration is the goal.

As for the first point, we should note that the term self-defense is somewhat of a misnomer. Wing Chun master Tony Massengill likes to remind his students that SWAT teams and Special Forces are never thinking of defense—they're always seeking to attack. Likewise, our stance is structured in such a way that we can launch either hand or foot without hesitation.

Also, the on-guard stance must be both rooted and mobile. Real fighting requires that the fighter is ready to both hit-and-move and fend off grappling/clinching attacks. There is, therefore, no "perfect" stance. Instead, the goal of the on-guard position is to be flexible (adaptable). In this regard, the JKD on-guard is a work of genius in that it readily allows the JKD fighter to function at all ranges of fighting. Too often JKD students branch off into other arts altogether because they misapprehend Lee's exhortation to "have no way as way". Clearly, they misunderstand this to mean that one should use different arts and methods. But in looking closely at the on-guard stance, we see a unique and crafty set-up that allows slight modifications at a moments notice in order to deal with the changing demands of combat.

For example, should it be called for, the stance can be elongated (similar to the Wing Chun Pole form) to give longer reach to the forward side. Just as well, a quick shift allows the stance to turn completely "open". Much confusion reigns in JKD circles because people try to be "unlimited" with technique rather than footwork, timing, and tactics. It's the latter, we should always remember, that makes a system "alive" and any stance/structure that grossly limits movement and/or discourages it is antithetical to scientific self-defense.

Defensively speaking, there is no way for any stance or technique to literally "cover" a fighter from every attack. But a proper and logical on-guard stance should positionally limit access to primary targets while not impeding one's own offensive opportunities—and this is precisely what the JKD on-guard stance endeavors to do. At long range, the leading hand and foot are "in-line", that is to say they are pointed—like a gun—at your opponent. This forms the primary structural design of JKD's interception philosophy. Any time the opponent is within range, he must defend himself from the rapid attacks of the rapier-like lead hand/foot of the JKD fighter. All footwork in JKD is designed to maneuver the fighter to a position where such counter/intercepting fire is feasible.

Hence, you can see how the JKD on-guard stance tries to achieve all three of the stance objectives in one quick, integrated package. Importantly, all three are of equal importance to the JKD fighter because to do one without reference to the others can lead to a structural breakdown and defeat. For example, a fighter that focuses too much on movement without maintaining "the line" in order to counter-attack and stop-hit might very well run out of room and be overrun.

In many systems the trainee is introduced to the stance and there is a kind of separation between the stance and the fighting techniques of the method. In JKD no such dichotomy exists. The on-guard/bi-jong is designed to be moved and fired from and there is no JKD stance without JKD striking. Bruce Lee himself said that, basically, all JKD practice was in some fashion or another ready-position practice—or, "small-phasic-bent-knee practice" as he referred to the on-guard stance.

On this point, a fighter's skill depends severely on how well he/she is able to maintain their balance when under the stress of all-out fighting. Many great fighters make combat look somewhat easier than it truly is because of this ability. Perhaps you've noticed when viewing an MMA or boxing match that the great pros—the St.Pierres, and Silvas, and Mayweathers—seem to have an easier time of it than novices. Indeed, the action seems to be more deliberate and controlled by the champions than the helter-skelter nature of the upstarts. This phenomenon was something that very much puzzled me when I first began studying the fighting arts many years ago. After all, you would think at first glance that the champions would be doing more than the novices when, in fact, it appeared they were doing less.

And this is just the thing! JKD is very much a science of movement—and what we're moving is the on-guard stance, not just our feet. Any attempt to study and practice JKD without focusing on its stance, footwork, and striking integration is utterly futile because it is this that is the core of Lee's method. He understood the volatile changes common to fighting and, consequently, sought to tame these intangibles by having a system designed to move. But not just any type of movement...movement that provided an optimal balance between offense and defense and that subsumed the other principles that we'll study more in-depth later.

Everyone will have slight variations of their ready position due to their unique physical structure. This doesn't mean, however, that we should eschew the primary principles of the stance. The knees should be slightly bent and the rear heel elevated only a little bit. The rear heel elevation allows for a more rapid closing of ground and helps facilitate the explosive twisting required when throwing the rear hand. Also, the heel can drop when need be for defensive purposes. A quick note: the knees always have to be bent but the rear heel doesn't always have to be elevated. The former is an absolute rule in that straight legs will not just be vulnerable to attack (the knees especially can be severely injured when locked) but will also make it nearly impossible to move quickly. But the latter rule is more flexible in that a fighter can still move well with their heels on the floor in some cases, and tactically, like the boxers of old, putting weight on the rear leg might be called for in some defensive situations.

All-out fighting requires both mobility and stability. You will need to move and you will need to be prepared in case your opponent grabs, shoves, or pulls you. Some confusion exists among JKD students on the point of grappling as they mistakenly conclude they need to abandon their JKD structure and adapt a grappling style because they are unrooted too easily when the fight goes to close quarters. But a proper understanding and practice of the on-guard stance can remedy this as it should give the JKD fighter both the agility and the rootedness needed. This is also why all JKD students should practice Wing Chun's first form properly as it trains the stance and legs to "grip" the floor and prevents the JKD fighter from being too one-dimensional in their stance. We should note that JKD starts with mobility training and endeavors to add structure to that movement, whereas Wing Chun starts with structure and progresses to movement.

There is perhaps no greater omission in fighting arts than that of footwork. For our purposes there must be constant effort put forth to fully integrate our stance and footwork. If you've been training at a Jeet Kune Do school that hasn't practiced, much less mentioned, footwork and stance lately, you're in the wrong place. Proper footwork is not fancy, it's the expeditious movement of the ready position to control distance, access a target, and/ or avoid being one. A JKD student should be constantly engaged in the practice of footwork because superior movement capacity allows a fighter to shut down any opponent's offense and secure their own attacks.

Boxing, wrestling, MMA, Muay Thai, and other competitive sports/arts have the advantage of alive training, i.e., practice that requires competition between students where there is constant footwork. In real fights people do not simply stand still. Any martial art that does not practice the integration of footwork with its techniques is dangerously deluded. The sooner you can add footwork (which is to say timing too, because to move properly one must be in-tune with the opponent) to your training the better.

Basically, there are four directions to move: forward, back, angling left, or angling right (whether to the front or rear). A side-step is somewhat of a misnomer as a fighter is actually angling rather than moving straight to the side--as in many cases (though not all) doing so would destroy proper alignment with the opponent. With these directions there are four types of physical footwork or, if you will, transportation, for the ready position. They are the step-slide, push-shuffle, slide-step, and the pivot.

The step-and-slide is where the foot closest to the direction you're moving steps forward and the other foot slides after it. This technique is generally the workhorse of one's footwork as it is the simplest, safest, and least energy-taxing. It is also a short movement, leaving the fighter in transit for the shortest period of time. Getting caught in transit is exceedingly dangerous as the fighter then has two problems—the attack AND their own balance. The push-shuffle covers about the same distance as a step-and-slide but the near foot doesn't step on its own power. Instead, the near foot is "pushed" by the other foot, which makes the push-shuffle a more explosive form of movement. Slide-steps are also very effective. To slide-step forward, slide the rear foot to the front and then step forward with the front. This needs to be done quickly, smoothly (with no hopping, which taxes the legs too much and can prematurely fatigue a fighter) and with discernment since it covers much more distance than the previous two motions. Finally, we have pivoting. A pivot is to swing one leg around in an arc while keeping the other foot at the same place but changing its angle of facing. Pivoting can be done with either leg and can be used by the expert to shift the angle of facing ever so slightly while also conserving ever precious energy. Unlike the other forms of footwork, a pivot can be very slight or much greater in its depth of movement depending upon the situation.

At first, practice of footwork should include these four separately, but the ultimate goal is to integrate them not merely in combination but also in single execution. For example, while stepping forward with a step-slide the situation could change instantly and call for the advancing fighter to reverse direction or angle. In such a case the step-slide could stop mid-step and a slide-step backwards or a pivot, angle-step (side-step) could be executed. Another common scenario is when moving backwards with a slide-step the rear foot, instead of retreating in a straight line, can swing out—thus forming a slide-pivot rather than a straight slide-step.

Also, and very importantly, footwork should be practiced with different cadences. A predictable rhythm is an accident waiting to happen. This isn't because sudden violent encounters are like boxing matches, necessarily, but because all people move with a slightly different rhythm. A master fighter is able to instantly "fit in" with their opponent--and this fitting in requires footwork that is quickly adaptable. A footwork master is capable of instantly judging the right distance and angle and attaining that position in as expeditious a manner as possible. Only constant practice can yield such skill.

It's rather common and, therefore, lamentable that virtually no one brags about the skill of a fighter's footwork. But with few exceptions, if a fighter is unable to out-position his opponent he must be stronger and more durable (or limit the engagement by unnatural rules). Again— good footwork isn't fancy, it simply gets you to where you can limit your opponent's offense by superior angling and position while maximizing your own offensive opportunities. Trying to score offensively without first having gained a positional advantage is the height of folly and fistic arrogance. Great fighters are careful and they always respect their opponent, knowing that they themselves can always be injured if caught flush. Confidence is knowing that if you get better position, you can finish anyone; arrogance is thinking you don't need position.

As mentioned, a critical aspect of footwork is timing. We'll cover all of this in greater detail in the volume on training, but suffice it to say that one cannot separate the right time from the right position. Timing, distance, and angle (position) are all happening simultaneously, though we are inclined to address them apart from each other for the sake of educational clarity. Frankly, there is no way possible to achieve all of these without a partner to train with and this should form the centerpiece of one's application training. Partner-training gets to the heart of what is called aliveness—which is, after all, simply one having so mastered their own technique that they are able to obliterate any thinking of themselves without an opponent. Incidentally, "proper" sparring in JKD should always have these issues first in mind. A fighter that develops an instinctive sense of space and time will excel at technique, but not the other way around. There is really no other way to develop this without boxing type training of some sort, i.e., sparring, bag work, working the mitts.

Much confusion about JKD would simply evaporate if there was proper understanding of footwork. In 1980 Sugar Ray Leonard fought the ferocious Roberto Duran and suffered his first professional defeat to the man known as "Hands of Stone." What's instructive here is that Leonard, the slick and speedy boxer, decided to stand and trade with Duran. Why? Well, he was apparently angry that Duran had made obscene gestures to his wife before the match. Fighting on toughness rather than skill, Leonard lost a close decision.

In the famous rematch later that year, Leonard didn't look like the same fighter. Knowing that Duran was a macho and aggressive man, Leonard boxed and moved and feinted and jabbed. The only similarity between the two matches was the name of the fighters. Leonard never stood still and gave Duran a chance to make the fight a brawl. Frustrated by his inability to catch the fleet-footed challenger and hammered by some well placed stiff jabs, Duran's ego got the better of him in the 8th round and he infamously declared, "no mas." He quit.

You see, Duran was an extraordinary boxer. He was undeniably an all-time great. He was exceedingly tough and durable too, but no tough fighter can do what's physically impossible: they can't hit what's not there. Good footwork in all-out fighting won't (and can't at times) look like Sugar Ray's performance that night in New Orleans but that doesn't mean that footwork isn't essential for success. Angling, shifting, pivoting... there is always space to move. In any fight there are three physical constants: you, the foe(s), and space. Always make it a two against one; use the space against him. A master of footwork never presents a good target. A master of footwork uses his feet to shut down the foe's offense by better positioning and then capitalizes on his mistakes. Heavy bags are fun to hit because they don't move. Don't fight like a heavy bag. And remember, the next time you hear an instructor talk about being "unlimited" or "having no way as way" in fighting, and they don't mention footwork, use your own—run as far away as possible.

Constant heavy bag practice, shadow boxing, sparring, jumping rope, working the mitts...these all give the JKD fighter, like the boxer, the intuitive feel for mobile balance. All of the philosophical utterances made by Lee about fighting and JKD can be understood in practice by great footwork—which, of course, implies the stance. Like the boxer, the JKD fighter knows that there is no stance without footwork and there is no stance/footwork without striking. They are all integrated.

In many JKD schools that misapprehend boxing's integral role in the art, I've noticed that the students are not led through "open" bag rounds (where they "work" the bag) with an emphasis on footwork and integration of offense/defense. They hit the bags like Rocky hit the meat—mindlessly, with no tactical direction. Or, worse still, instructors have them practice footwork in dead "line-drills", but this is like trying to help a student write a novel by bringing him to spelling bees. Great footwork IS fistic freedom! Go check out the boxing masters of old and liberate yourself from overly complicated ramblings of those that think a fight is a set piece battle. Watch the underrated Gene Tunney hit with power from both hands while moving, moving, moving and clinching too (and imagine if he could have used Wing Chun from the clinch too!). Jack Johnson, Driscoll, Ali, Robinson, Julio Cesar Chavez, the incomparable Willie Pep, Pernell Whitaker...all mobile and deadly—and unique too. Don't try and reinvent the wheel. Study the boxing masters of old and you will see for yourself what we've discussed in this section and hopefully you'll be inspired, your passions will stir, and you'll get back into your workouts with a renewed vigor. Think about this: in the *Game of Death* when Bruce Lee is giving Dan Inosanto a beating, he's admonishing him for his refusal to see beyond "rehearsed routines" and dead patterns. Take careful note, beyond the cinematic trappings and Lee's inimitable charisma, that he was simply boxing with his footwork. Yes, indeed, that's the physical vehicle he was using to express those deep ideas about aliveness and fitting in with an opponent.

So, if you find yourself discouraged by all the esoteric blather written and taught about Mr. Lee, think about this simple truth and box...just box and you'll begin to get it. It's simple--not easy--but you can get it with the right focus and enough practice. It all comes down to footwork.

THE STRAIGHT LEAD AND JAB

If there is any one blow that we can point to and say, "There! See...that is the essence of JKD," it is certainly the leading straight punch or, if you will, the jab. It is perfectly brutal and simple exactly because it is so scientific. The straight lead is all but an

abandoned tool, buried at the bottom of most fighter's tool box underneath weapons they esteem more highly like the hook and round kicks. But these are grossly misapplied in the absence of the stiff, swift, terrible jab.

The great boxing master, Driscoll says it best: "...let him realize that boxing is the noble art of self-defense, that it has always borne that name and that its practice and study is still recommended on this sole plea. He should also remember, however, that defense is not only the chief thing to be considered but that attack can only be allowed to come into the picture at all when it is employed as an auxiliary to defense and that the strongest form of defense is a vigorous attack, carried out mainly and almost entirely with a view to the minimizing of the risk, or the repulse, of all counter-attack...Now as most people are aware, the very first principle of fencing is that the student must learn to keep the line. For as long as he can contrive to preserve a straight wall of steel in a direct line from his shoulder down to his arm, so long will his body be impregnable to attack."

Driscoll also said, "A genuine straight left should not only pull up an attacking opponent in his stride but at the same time jar him to his heels. It should be so well timed as to reach its mark at the utmost of its owner's power, that is, with the maximum reach at his command."

With this said, it should be clear that neither Driscoll, nor Lee, thought of this punch as merely a "jab" but as a full-on, robust and damaging blow. Lee knew that the Wing Chun straight punch was both structurally and tactically the most sound punch he could throw but, not having finished his Wing Chun training with Chum Kui, the Mook Jong, and Bui Jee—all forms that added power and footwork to his Sil Lim Tao structure—he saw Driscoll's (and Dempsey's) lead punch as the natural answer to this limitation. In the *Fighting Method* series Lee actually points out that both the long straight lead and the short lead of Wing Chun are used interchangeably in JKD depending upon the range. This is one of our strongest pieces of evidence that Lee himself never saw the two methods as against one another. He never abandoned his Wing Chun; he added bare-knuckle boxing to it.

More Driscoll: "Do not dab, but hit fiercely and determinedly with each delivery, always aiming for the center of the face...Go after your man. Send out that left straight and true and hard...For no matter how unpolished or unscientific he [your foe] may be, he can always afford to disregard a pushing or tapping left, and without wasting time or energy in defense, can force his way in to certain victory."

Driscoll, like Dempsey, taught that a true straight lead, or jolt, was the most powerful of all blows, and the fact that it wasn't viewed as such by most boxers was evidence of their lack of true fistic education rather than an actual deficit in the lead. On this point Driscoll wrote: "While the young boxer may be ready and willing to accept the fact that the straight left is the speediest of all punches, simply because it has the shortest distance to travel, it is often difficult for him to appreciate the relative power of straight and round arm hitting. To him it seems so certain that a swing must necessarily be so much more forceful than a straight delivery and there is a lot of reason for this mistaken belief. The sensation of vigor suggested by a full revolution of the arm and the further sensation that every ounce of the weight of the body is being carried behind it as though it were being all thrown at the recipient, is so fascinating that he cannot resist the notion that a swinging punch must automatically be the more powerful."

So, most young boxers/martial artists will go on in their education assuming that straight hitting is less powerful than swinging strikes. But this is anatomically impossible since a true straight has the whole structural force of the body behind it. A swinger has success against other such rivals and "feeble" jabbers but should he run up against a master of the jab he is doomed as it is both the fastest and the hardest blow available in punching.

It's helpful to quote Dempsey at length on this point:

"I use the expression 'left jolt' instead of 'left jab' because I don't want you to confuse the type of straight left you will throw, with the futile straight left or 'jab' used by most current boxers. Most of them couldn't knock your hat off with their left jabs. With their lefts they tap, they slap, they flick, they paw, they 'paint'. Their jabs are used more to confuse than to stun.

"Their jabs are used as fluttering defensive flags to prevent their poorly instructed opponents from 'getting set to punch'. A good fighter doesn't have to 'get set'. He's always ready to punch. Some of them use their jabs merely to make openings for their rights. And that's dangerously silly, for the proper brand of feinting would accomplish the same purpose. With but few exceptions, they do not use the left jab as a smashing jolt that can be an explosive weapon by itself—that can knock you down or knock you out.

"There are two reasons why the left jolt is a rarity in fighting today. First, nearly all current boxers launch their jabs with the non-step shoulder whirl. Secondly, nearly all have been fed the defensive hokum that it's less dangerous to try to tap an opponent with the left than to knock him down.

"Concerning that defensive hokum, let me say this: any time you extend your left fist either for a tap or for an all-out punch, you're taking a gamble on being nailed with a counter-punch. And the sap who uses 'light stuff'—rapping, flicking, etc.—has his left hand extended much more often than the explosive left jolter, who doesn't waste punches, doesn't shoot until he has feinted or forced his opponent into an opening. It's true that you can 'recover' your balance more quickly after missing a tap than after missing a hard punch. But it's also true that an opponent who is defending only against taps and slaps will be much more alert to counter than will an opponent who is being bombed."

I must admit my love of Dempsey's language here. Bombed, he says! And he is spot on; a powerful jolt is an indispensable weapon for the smart fighter who knows that being smart and scientific doesn't mean passivity. Without mastery of the jolt, the JKD fighter is forced, rather naturally, to develop all sorts of back-up skills to compensate.

Parenthetically, this is something for the Wing Chun fighter to consider as well. All too often you will see WC students throwing slappy blasts with no real power as they rush ahead to learn every sao under the sun, forgetting Ip Man's assertion that the best bridge technique was a punch in the nose.

For precisely this reason the jab and straight hitting form the nucleus of JKD striking. Of the multitude of methods one can study for self-defense, you should take careful notice of the absence of straight hitting in virtually all of them except for Wing Chun, old boxing, and JKD. Interestingly, as simple as this notion may appear to be, it is decidedly difficult to master since people are natural "swingers"(which is to say they throw haymakers, not that they're in "open" marriages). Driscoll called these attacks the work of "bear-cat brawlers" in that they resembled the fighting structure of animals rather than men. But, of course, men do not have claws so wild swats aren't nearly as effective for us as they are for, say, bears.

On a side note, you will notice here the close family resemblance of JKD/ Wing Chun/Bare Knuckle Boxing and, moreover, clear physical evidence of my argument that JKD is rather simply a combat expression of the Wing Chun concept. This is to say that it's an art built on Wing Chun principles and adapted and expressed in certain combative environments.

The straight lead can be thrown as a power punch or as a speed jab depending upon the tactical necessity of the situation. Dempsey's critique against light rapping and painting shouldn't lead us off in the wrong (opposite) direction. A speed jab can certainly be used to good effect in many situations should the need arise. The danger is in thinking that this is all the lead hand is good for. A slight hunch of the hip, extension of the shoulder and deeper penetration of the blow can turn what looks like a simple jab into a power jab—or, if you will, a straight lead. This deceptively simple punch is the cornerstone of the fighting machine that is JKD. It isn't one of many blows we might throw, it's the main blow and to throw another strike is to imply that this primary one was unavailable at that precise moment.

It is thrown with the palm to the side (unlike in contemporary boxing) because this allows the fist to land squarely. A broken hand is the desultory result of landing a punch the wrong way. Furthermore, the JKD lead punch is integrated into the on-guard stance to allow rapid delivery and recovery. To deviate from this structure is to abandon JKD altogether. (Remember: faking, footwork, and timing are what make the JKD fighter alive and "unlimited", not doing other methods that contradict our core principles). And, since the shoulder is a ball-and-socket joint, once we turn the palm down or elevate the elbow, we've disconnected the punch from our structural source.

A simple experiment will convince you of the efficacy of this structure. Extend a straight punch and cup it with your free hand. Push back into the punch with the cupped hand. With your fist vertical you will feel virtually no stress in your shoulder joint. Once you turn your pam downward, however, you will notice a considerable strain. Also, as noted, the vertical fist structure is safer to strike with than a horizontal fist as the knuckles of the fingers and your wrist are better protected at impact.

One should also note too that a martial artist is training to protect and preserve. Damaging yourself in training is somewhat contradictory to this end. The number one injury in boxing today is hands—not face. This occurs even though the boxers wear hand-wraps and large gloves scientifically designed to protect them. How much worse will it be for your bare hands should you adapt their methods for self-defense?

Train to keep the elbow from flaring outward as you throw the punch. Launch it with snap, not push, but be careful throwing it in the air, as in when shadowboxing, because this may lead to elbow injury. As with all striking, a heavy bag is a tremendous asset for training. Take care to find the proper range when working on the heavy bag, though. Standing too close will teach you to "push" the punch and too far away and, ouch, you might hurt your elbow. The proper range is where you can score and have another inch or two for follow-through. Train vigorously to stay as loose as possible and to develop speed, speed, and more speed. A bullet, after all, is simply a piece of lead. If I threw it at you, I'd be a jerk; if I whip it at you through a sling-shot, I'm guilty of assault; if I fire it at you through a gun, I'm a murderer. The difference between the three isn't the lead, it's the speed. Speed kills. Hitting power comes from good form done fast, with proper intent, follow-through, position and timing. There's no such thing as a knock-out push.

The straight punch can be thrown as a counter or a lead and, when using it tactically, may even be used as a form of faking. Shortening it and throwing it only as a quick jab—not intending to land fully—might set your foe up for a heavier strike—especially a kick. Because of its swiftness, the lead punch is your best friend in fighting—always ready to strike. It's educated use is the sign of an intelligent fighter. A master of the straight lead/JKD jab is able to throw this punch from any position and is always looking for ways to use it as it is simply the safest strike a human being can possibly throw. Often, sparring is used to compete when, in fact, a studious fighter uses it as an opportunity to develop footwork and timing so as to dominate with this "basic" strike. Moreover, much confusion in JKD arises when this brilliant stroke is minimized in training for whatever reasons.

As previously mentioned, a prime reason many JKD schools have little use for the JKD jab is because they believe that its simplicity requires great speed and timing to deliver, which not all fighters possess. On the face of this there is a plausible premise— many of us aren't as fast as Bruce Lee—but the conclusion drawn is erroneous. Since I'm not as fast as Bruce Lee, does that mean I should do something more complex than he did (since nothing is more simple than the straight lead)? Doesn't complexity require even more speed than a simpler movement? This whole business of Lee being a better athlete than everyone else is somewhat overblown—bordering on idolatry. His speed was not such that it trumped the laws of physics and, with that in mind, a straight punch is still the fastest punch in any arsenal, regardless of one's speed.

Surely, if I was in a gun fight and my opponent had a larger gun than mine, that doesn't mean that I still can't kill him with the smaller weapon. And it certainly doesn't imply that I should drop my "inferior" handgun and go for a stick! The straight lead is the most advanced (though simple looking) weapon on the planet for use in hand-to-hand combat.

A variation of the lead is the leading finger jab, which targets, of course, the eye of your opponent. Great care must be taken in practice to develop accuracy, for not only does the eye-jab go after a small target, that target is surrounded by bone. A miss can damage your finger so it should be used sparingly and swiftly, as a tap, a touch, or a flick rather than as a spear. Practicing on the BOB bag is helpful.

Another variation that I personally find no use for is the back-fist. True enough, Lee used it himself but the back-fist has many dangers we should consider.

First, it's very easy to miss and strike with the back of your hand rather than the back of the knuckles. Smacking the back of your hand into hard bone is a very easy way to break your hand. Furthermore, since it travels a curved path it isn't as fast as the lead punch, doesn't have as much power and isn't as accurate. With the exception of throwing a back-fist against the back of your foe's guard hand (trying to injure it and/or move it off the line) there is much more risk than reward for the back-fist. Even worse still, there are some JKD instructors teaching something called a power back-fist, which is such a bad idea as to be nearly insane. There is simply no way to "toughen" up the bones on the back of your hand and should you launch a "heavy" back-fist and collide with the top of your foe's head you'll likely shatter your hand so bad as to reduce your use of that hand permanently.

CROSS OR REAR STRAIGHT PUNCH

All of this talk of the efficacy of the jab should not lead us down the path of thinking that—marvelous as it is—it's an end in and of itself. An all-out fight, absent of a designated start time and ideal footing, is no boxing match. In the Sil Lim Tao form, the Wing Chun student learns to throw the straight punch with either hand. This should be our guide. Boxing, as much as it is derived from fencing, does not put a sword in our hands. Thus, no matter how "sharp" your jab is, it's still not a rapier, and to miss this critical distinction between fist-fighting and sword play can cause the gross error of over reliance upon the lead. Fighters who rely too much on their lead hand have a tendency to close their stance off too much. Teri Tom, a Ted Wong protege, in her otherwise fantastic book (which I heartily recommend), *The Straight Lead*, makes exactly this mistake.

In trying to stay close to the fencing roots of old-boxing, Ms. Tom deems the "long" stance, with the lead shoulder fully forward, as superior to Wing Chun's more squared stance since the lead punch has more range when the lead shoulder is in that advanced position. But at the end of Chum Kui, the Wing Chun fighter is throwing exactly this kind of "long-bridge" lead punch—and, what's more—with either hand. The stance is fluid, after all. Slight movements and adjustments are essential in fighting. A JKD fighter should be able to turn the lead shoulder fully forward to launch the jab from as extended a position as possible, but he must also be able to get that rear punch in as well.

In a hurry to distance JKD from Wing Chun, Ms. Tom blurs the distinction between the jab and the rapier. Sure, our jab should be rapier like but it can't actually kill someone (unless you're George Foreman!). Therefore, the ability to quickly engage the rear hand— either in attack or for bridging/clinching—is absolutely essential. Driscoll himself said that clinching is a part of footwork. And Dempsey, no weak puncher, warned of the dreadful dangers of in-fighting in street fights. Wing Chun, is a science of in-fighting and is, thus, more suited to the actual demands of all-out fighting than boxing in this regard. This being the case, we should assiduously avoid closing off our stance too much and endeavor to maintain a "facing" stance.

In Wing Chun we say that we often have a leg forward but not really a side forward. I think we can look at this in spirit if not always to the letter of the law. The rear punch or cross should be able to instantly join the fray for the JKD fighter and should be thrown with the same arm mechanics as the lead. A twist of the shoulder and hip will be needed to give it the distance as well as extra pop.

The cross in JKD is structurally a rear straight punch, not the looping overhand type blow that you often see and which is mistaken as the rear cross. It is heavy artillery as it gathers a great amount of momentum, and though it's thrown with the weaker rear hand, it can end matters instantly. Placing the strong hand forward as we do in "conventional" JKD makes developing this blow important, and it will take hours of practice to be able to throw it loosely, with power and proper form. The temptation to be avoided is to lean over at the waist and loop the rear hand at the target. This common mistake handicaps the rear cross to the point that its great advantages are lost entirely.

The rear cross should be thrown as straight as possible, with the arm and shoulder loose—allowing the punch to whip to the target and back. As with all power punches, aim an inch or two past the target. Special care must be taken in practice to develop "speed-power" rather than "push power". What this means is that there is often a psychological drag on the musculature when trying to deliver a powerful blow that causes us to tense up, which has a rather deleterious effect on the whole enterprise. Tension will actually cause the punch to lose power because it's moving slower. Plus, and not to be understated, is that any excess tension will cause us to fatigue prematurely and once you're too tired your training is of no avail. We do well to watch the effect of tension on novice fighters in shows like *The Ultimate Fighter* (though I don't recommend the program for much else). Many of the participants are able to train for long hours without running down but then, astonishingly, they are grossly fatigued in a matter of minutes in an actual match. Obviously they're in very good shape, but what we're witnessing is not just nerves but also the effect of trying to throw strikes too hard.

As with the lead, endeavor to keep your elbow down and fist vertical. Many fighters throw the cross with the elbow up, flared to the outside, and they lean over their front leg, moving their shoulders down. This has many disadvantages—chief amongst them is the disruption of balance and destruction of the on-guard stance. Most fighters do this because they can't reach their foe, so instead of using fakes and footwork to gain the proper distance they lean forward and throw what is essentially an overhand punch. Plus, when you move your shoulders towards the floor you've effectively disconnected the fist from its power source—or power-line, leaving the punch weaker and the hand/wrist more susceptible to injury.

The cross gets its name from the fact that it's supposed to "cross over the middle" or "cross over the opponent's jab". Obviously, one can use the rear hand with devastating effect even with the elbow flared out slightly, kind of going around the middle, but the JKD fighter should see this as an adaptation rather than a rule. Surely, if the opponent is open for the wider blow and it can be thrown safely, one should let it fly. But this should be seen in the context of the straighter blow being already jammed, for the more one opens up their strikes, as the great Dempsey once said, the more they open up their own defense.

The JKD cross should be thrown with the toe, knee, hip, shoulder and knuckles all facing the target exactly at impact. There should be no wind-up but to properly add power to the cross there should be a slight "arc" at the end of the blow. Naturally the body wants to wind-up and throw a haymaker, and this will, indeed, give you a fairly significant punch. The downside is, of course, that you are quite an inviting target throughout and especially after the blow. In JKD, with the integrity of our on-guard stance being paramount, our cross should be thrown with maximum whip—not pushing—and the blow should snap an inch or two past the target (never stopping) before whipping in a tight, almost imperceptible circle back to scratch. Be diligent not to over-commit the hip and shoulder; they should not pass the punching line as to do so leaves us exposed, wastes energy, and makes throwing another strike that much more difficult. Remember: the longer you are away from your ready position, the longer you're exposed to counter fire and the less options you have for defense. Not only does the smart fighter endeavor to minimize the amount of movement they make in a violent encounter where seconds and inches count, they also train diligently to avoid being an accessible target. Prevention is better than cure and the better your offense--that is to say, the more controlled it is—the less work your defense has to do. It's somewhat like in American football: a fumble or interception by the offense gives the defense a most thankless task and no offense is good if it scores points but turns the ball over too much.

SNAP KICK

The snap kick can be thrown with either leg but the front (closest) is preferred as it offers more range—and the further away you can be from your opponent while hurting him the better, methinks. But, nevertheless, either leg will do depending on the position you have to your foe.

The snap kick is a most simple tool to use and yet terribly vexing to your enemy—especially those in an open-stance that expose their groin. Many fighters today, dangerously, stand with their groin fully exposed. Worse still, they throw kicks with a wind-up (Muay Thai style) and have virtually no defense against groin attacks. True, today's fighters appear to be significantly more dangerous due to the proliferation of MMA style schools, but they are somewhat handicapped because they ignore some of the realities of all-out fighting. Very formidable, these MMA stylists are rather reckless in exposing themselves to damaging blows landed in the most vulnerable areas. All-out fighting—where every part of the body is a weapon and target—is a careful, careful game, not to be engaged in helter-skelter style as one well placed blow, even by a weaker foe, can severely complicate matters in a hurry.

The JKD snap kick, whipping off the floor straight at the target, is a kick that is a perpetual threat to the foe's lead leg and groin. It can be landed with the top of the foot, ball of the foot or even the toe if wearing proper shoes and thrown at the groin or chin. With good shoes on, this strike is particularly effective because the shoes are somewhat like a set of brass knuckles for the feet. The goal is to keep the knee low as the kick shovels off the floor. The leg should be extended about three quarters as it advances to the target. At the last second it should whip upward with snap from the loose leg. The whip effect should carry through impact and the leg should accelerate even into the recovery phase. As with all JKD weapons, the integrity of the on-guard position is critically important and the student should practice this kick tirelessly until they've gained the habit of snapping the leg like a jab and can recover in an instant.

Since the leg is so much heavier than the arm, the emphasis in kicking should be on snap and speed. An impressive amount of power can be delivered without sacrificing too much balance and recovery when the JKD student has mastered this simple but important kick. Like the straight lead/jab, it can be thrown with disconcerting swiftness. And, like the other kicks of JKD, the secret is in not chambering or drawing the foot back before the kick to gain power. Power in JKD kicking comes from the speed of the kick and the intent should be to "shovel" it to the target and disguise your intent. Since the snap kick derives its power from the straight line momentum, it doesn't require that the knee be raised first (artificially anyway) since the knee is already above the foot anatomically. This being the case, defending against the snap kick can prove to be a daunting task. It can be especially devastating when used against an immobile, predictable opponent. Every JKD student should endeavor to master their footwork to the point that they are able to keep this kick and their jab on the attack incessantly -offering their rival no respite.

When kicking with the lead leg, if range requires it, the rear foot should slide forward quickly and the kicking leg should leave the floor—at the latest—as soon as the rear foot reaches its new spot. Always, there should be careful practice put into not telegraphing the delivery which very often comes from the back foot hopping towards the front rather than sliding. Unless the upper body stays perfectly still and level the opponent cannot help but see the kick coming.

Even still, though, no matter how fast one's kick is, the feet are never as swift as the hands so leading with kicks can prove to be a frustrating—even dangerous endeavor. Instead, aim to use the snap kick as a finish to a combination, after a fake, or as a counter as this will minimize the risk of you being countered.

In his day, Bruce Lee was confronted primarily by Karate stylists who were using more closed stances than today's MMA/Muay Thai stylists do, so he didn't emphasize this simple beauty too much. In his on-screen fight with Bob Wall in *Way of the Dragon*, however, we see a perfect example of using the snap kick (he actually throws it from behind Mr. Wall). Just as with the jab and cross, both the front and rear snap kicks should be practiced diligently. With "having no way as way" in mind, one can see multiple uses for this tool. An opponent who keeps a wide guard with his weight forward might be kicked underneath the chin by either leg's snap kick. This could be used to terrible effect with certain footwear to aid the impact.

LEAD TO THE BODY

Many times in fighting, the novice abandons the straight lead and cross simply because the opponent's head is momentarily covered or unreachable. The smart fighter, however, one who believes in the efficacy of straight hitting, seeks to make the body a target for his straight blows as well as the head. And there is good reason for this since—as the old boxing proverb says, "there's a foot of body for every inch of chin". Of course, this saying originated back in a day before the proliferation of fast food so perhaps it can be rightly updated to read, "there's a mile of flab for every inch of hard head".

To throw the lead punch to the body, the JKD fighter should lower his center of gravity slightly by bending his knees and driving his weight toward his foe's center of mass. The fist, as Dempsey would say, gets all the glory but is really just along for the ride as it slams into the foe's ribs, stomach or low abdomen. The emphasis should be on "dropping" your weight and "sticking" the punch into the bad guy's gut. A straight body punch isn't thrown with snap (or whip as with a hook to the body) but must dig into the target as boxers say. The danger in this, we should note, is that the lead to the body, not being thrown with the same snap as the lead to the head, can turn into a slower punch if we're not careful. But just because the punch requires a dig into the target doesn't mean it's a push-punch. Acceleration is still the key but just with a little more emphasis on driving the blow.

Stepping forward with the lead leg—thereby extending one's reach—

can greatly aid in the delivery of this under-appreciated blow. The back foot should push the lead side of the body forward and the lead foot should land only after the blow has landed or else the momentum created by the step is wasted. The rear hand should be carried high and ready for any defensive assistance needed.

Some debate exists over whether at impact this blow should land with the vertical or horizontal fist alignment. While there is very low risk of breaking one's hand when striking the body (watch the elbows and hip bones, though) there is still the issue of the shoulder being a ball-and-socket joint. The vertical fist alignment is always anatomically best for the shoulder/structure when throwing straight blows and going to the body doesn't change this fact. What isn't as much of a necessity is protecting the knuckles from damage from hard facial bones. This being the case, using the horizontal fist is permissible though not preferred. In either event, the JKD fighter should be careful to sink down enough with his body so that his shoulder is behind the punch at impact. Failure to do so not only weakens the blow but increases vulnerability to the wrist joint.

At the end of the blow, the punching hand should drop slightly— not curve as in the lead to the head—to "shorten the arc." This variation is due to the fact that the bodyweight is thrusting downward rather than slightly up and to the side with the earlier blow.

CROSS TO THE BODY

Perhaps no power blow in all of fighting is as neglected as the cross to the body. With too much emphasis placed on punching people only in the face, we forget how effective a well placed body blow can be. And not only this, an opponent that only needs to guard his face from punches is invariably faster than one that has more real-estate under assault. This punch is a cagey counter to wild attacks aimed at your head since it requires you to lower your center of gravity, which moves your head out of the path of the incoming blow. Not only this, but you also gain access to the exposed ribs of the puncher.

Be careful not to sway too far to the outside when delivering the cross to the body as this will make recovery more difficult. Deliver the punch simultaneously with a bend of the knees and waist—ever so slightly—and a quick, violent turn of the rear hip and shoulder. All must be accomplished at once for you to deliver the blow with good structure. As with the regular cross, aim to have the toe, knee, hip, shoulder and fist all facing the target at impact. At completion, follow-through and let the hand arc slightly. Unlike the straight lead to the body there doesn't need to be a downward motion to the shortened arc because the twist of the rear hip and shoulder are powering the blow more than the weight drop.

This punch is one of the most punishing blows in the hand tool set and a fighter that is unprepared to defend his body can be easily dispatched by its skillful execution. It is especially effective after a high jab or high fake when the opponent is leaning away from the head shot. Bare knuckles on the ribs are significantly more damaging than a blow with a boxing glove and might very well cause a fracture.

Many fighters mistakenly believe that having a multitude of techniques is what makes them dangerous but fighting isn't a game that rewards complexity and one should focus on simplicity, simplicity, simplicity. Furthermore, as we've covered, a loss of balance during fighting can be catastrophic and since straight blows disrupt our balance less than roundhouse/hook blows, these should be preferred and mastered. Also, the primary task of fighting is self-defense and good offense is one that doesn't compromise our defensive responsibilities. Straight hits like the lead and cross to both the head and body aid us defensively (are good offense) especially because they never leave us too open. As Driscoll points out, "there are only two ways to get through straight hits: you don't throw them, or you throw them and they're not straight."

Let us pause here to consider for a moment the type of attacks that you are likely to face in real life. If you are unfortunate enough to find yourself on the receiving end of a physical assault, you can be very certain that your opponent won't be throwing too many straight blows at you, moving around much, feinting, and so forth. No...he'll be swinging with all his might—and these swings, despite our condemnation of them as unscientific blows, can still separate you from consciousness if they connect solidly. We shouldn't be confused on this point, nor should we be "martial-snobs", looking down over our scientific ready positions with scorn at our foe's amateurish tactics. A good martial artist is one that is confident through preparation, not someone that has no respect for his opponent. Another way of seeing this is to say that a confident fighter knows that if he executes properly he is prepared for any attack; an arrogant fighter thinks he cannot be defeated.

Careful practice on the heavy bags as well as shadow boxing should be done daily so that the JKD student is able to freely move and fire his basic attacks with control, speed and power. The wild attacks that will come at you by the average assailant will have murder on them— therefore, train to make these straight punches pure and mean too.

Resist the temptation to start throwing a multitude of combinations until you have the knack for landing these basic beauties with authority and balance. Mastery isn't doing something right once—it's doing something right so many times that you can't do it wrong anymore.

FRONT & REAR (STRAIGHT) KICK

Sometimes we refer to these punishing blows as the jab and cross kick and they're the workhorse of JKD's lower body tools. Thrown with the bottom of the feet (heel or ball of foot) these kicks are incredibly valuable assets in one's arsenal. With or without shoes on, the bottom of the foot is much better prepared to withstand impact damage than is the top of the foot. Thai boxers spend hours conditioning their legs to deliver their beloved round kick. The JKD fighter spends no time attempting to overcome nature's plan, preferring to hit with parts of the body best designed for it.

There is literally no part of the body that isn't a target for these two kicks but, obviously, the legs and low abdomen are inviting targets that are rather hard to defend. To throw the straight kicks, imagine throwing the JKD lead punch while your arms are dangling at your sides rather than up in a ready position. You wouldn't chamber the fist or bring it in to the center first, you'd simply raise your arm and throw the punch without preemptive movement. Well, this is exactly what we should have in mind for the straight kicks too though, naturally, to throw the front kick we'll have to slide the rear foot forward first if range is needed. Nevertheless, the mechanics of the two are very similar as the relation between the hip/shoulder, elbow/knee, and fist/foot are to be remembered. The straight kicks are, therefore, very natural to throw because—like the straight punch—they take advantage of the structural design of the large joint involved (hip).

Contact can be made with either the ball of the foot or the heel. Kicking with the ball of the foot requires more muscular force and momentum generation than landing with the heel. The JKD fighter should practice kicking either way so as to understand fully the pros and cons of both approaches. Landing with the ball of the foot requires a snap of hip to drive through the target and this can cause a disruption of balance. Landing with the heel, however, keeps the hip in a more rooted state and thus it's easier to advance after throwing the kick.

CHAIN PUNCHING

At this point you might very well be excused for believing that your JKD education has yielded a scant four punches—or worse still...just two with variations of height. Yes, you'd be excused for wondering this but you would actually have arrived at precisely that point in your training where the benefits of simplicity and straight hitting begin to merge. This merger leads us to something called chain punching.

Chain punching isn't just throwing a series of boxing style one-two's--as these are delivered primarily from the shoulder and move side-to-side and JKD delivers its barrage one over the top of the last, right from the center. As you see in the photos, the elbows stay in toward the body and each punch is thrown as straight as possible. Flaring the elbows out will cause the punches to curve in from the side and expose the body. The shoulders and hips will turn slightly with each blow to add power and reach but the weight must remained centered. Leaning forward at the waist will rob you of most of the benefits of the chain punching. First, it will weaken the blows

by turning your structural power-line (hip and shoulder) towards the floor instead of at your foe, make footwork more difficult and bring your face closer to your opponent's fists. Instead, get your distance from your footwork and power from torque and proper structural alignment.

The JKD blast as this is also known is not only several straight punches alternating between right and left. It can also be delivered with the jab hand alternately throwing two or more successive strikes in between the rear straight punch. Usually, though, a quick eruption of three, four or five blistering fast straight blows will do the job. This attack is especially effective when followed up by a low-line kick or push.

Also, by adding a quick blow to the body, the JKD chain blast is a very versatile combination, and there is no other form of punching that is as fast from such a distance. Bruce Lee smartly made this a staple of his punching arsenal.

To perfect the delivery of the blast, careful attention should be paid to the ending of the Sil Lim Tao form, which is where this unique combination comes from. It's been my experience that students that do not know and/or practice SLT can never quite get the knack of punching in this rarefied way. The vertical fist chain punching at the end of Wing Chun's first form—or lin wan kuen—is practiced with the shoulders square and that may seem contradictory to the JKD way but, remember, JKD is a variation of Wing Chun and not vice-versa. Consistent practice of SLT will, therefore, greatly assist the JKD student in developing the right body, hand, and elbow position required to master straight hitting.

Proper practice of SLT will give the JKD student skill at elbow positioning, centerline control, and last second energy, which are all essential to developing Bruce Lee type punches. Should you eschew learning and practicing this essential form, you'll more than likely find that when you attempt the straight blast your will elbows flare out—exposing your centerline—and that you end up pushing rather than snapping your punches. Also, you will likely engage in the habit of having your punching hand retract all the way to your face rather than the wu-sao guard position. Doing the latter, as in the SLT form, allows for better control of the opponent's bridge, quicker recycling of punches, and better defensive structure. This last point is especially needed in a day when grapplers seem to be ubiquitous and if your guard hand retracts to your face rather than your center you'll have less space with which to defend grabs/tackles.

Chain punching absolutely must be trained with footwork. A favorite drill of ours at The Academy is "open" focus mitts where the feeder (mitt holder) moves around, launches some attacks and rushes to be sidestepped/evaded by the student, and holds for a variation of blasts—some going forward or back and others swerving right, left or off the pivot. Again, sometimes because of the range involved and the fact that the opponent is moving this way or that, the forward hand (jab) might fire multiple times before the rear hand engages. Chain punching isn't 1-2-1-2; it's any series of uninterrupted straight hits. The master develops a knack for knowing his/her range and can throw these swift and vicious blows long or short depending on the need.

HOOK KICKS

JKD's lead leg hook kick is basically a sideways snap kick and is thrown with the hips closed relative to the opponent and the knee facing to the side. And, just like with the other kicks, to throw the lead leg kick, slide the rear forward and raise the knee in one fluid motion. The JKD hook kick should be thrown as straight to the target as possible and the real challenge in training is avoiding the wind-up by pulling the foot back to load it up (something you see quite often

in MMA today). As always, any telegraphic movements are to be expunged through diligent practice.

One modification we've made at our Academy in these past years is a lowering of JKD's reliance on this kick from Lee's time. Karate fighters of Lee's day usually blocked kicks either with their hands or by moving away from them. Today's MMA/Muay Thai style fighters are trained to "check" a leg kick, which basically means that they intend to block your leg kick with their shin bone against yours. Personally, I'm not quite fond of slamming my shin into other hard objects so limiting the use of this kick to times where the opponent doesn't have that option seems like a reasonable idea.

In *Bruce Lee's Fighting Method* series, the JKD hook kick is referred to as the most dominant kick in JKD and it is, save for this issue, quite an effective weapon in our tool box. But with the change of defensive tactics over the years, it is reasonable to adjust the use of the kick so as not to be clanging shins with people who, well, don't mind clanging shins. Also, with the changing times, more fighters today are squared up and looking to grapple. This makes the hook kick less effective than it was against karate fighters in that it will more than likely target the outside of the body rather than the more vulnerable middle and leave our own center exposed to counter-attack.

Today's fighter is indubitably more well-rounded and dangerous than the old karate student thanks to the UFC. There is, however, another sport-leak problem that the JKD fighter can seek to exploit when using the hook kick. Most MT/MMA fighters work to some degree on checking kicks. A slight modification of the hook kick can be made to use the shoe (sole or toe depending upon your footwear) to punish your foe who isn't trained to deal with that. (I still can't quite agree with anyone who's approach to self-defense is to deaden nerves on their body so that they can absorb damage when there are other, less painful options—like stop-hitting or moving.) French Savate makes great use of the shoe as a weapon and, indeed, it can be quite a game-changer for the fighter so inclined.

Against such a fighter, a nifty tactic is to draw the leg check response by faking a round/hook kick and then, when they take the bait, attack their now exposed groin with the snap kick.

The rear leg hook kick—or round kick—is quite a powerful weapon and one that is heavily appreciated in many systems. In Muay Thai, for example, the round kick is fearsome tool. They, of course, throw it up and down the body—attacking the leg, body and head...and they swing it like a bat as opposed to Tae Kwon Do which uses more snap from the knee. Either way, their round kick can be a devastating blow—especially since it lands often with the shin bone rather than the foot.

In JKD, with our emphasis on non-telegraphic motion, straight hitting, and soft targets, the rear leg isn't used as much as the closer lead side. Like any tool, it has its place such as when the opponent moves directly into the path of the rear leg. We should, after all, be able to use any tool at any time should the need arise. But in saying this, and in acknowledging the considerable power this kick offers, we must pause to note its considerable disadvantages.

First, it's a little harder to conceal the rear leg kick from the opponent. It can be used superbly at the end of a combination or as a counter kick but, as always, we must endeavor to set our man up, not throw it recklessly. If our opponent is inclined to grapple, this weapon might actually help him succeed in getting a good takedown since it puts the kicker in a rather precarious position. Often, even if you land the blow, you're quite off balance and the center of your body is exposed, which could cause more trouble than its worth and perhaps a straighter kick could have been delivered to better effect. Always a good guiding principle should be to ask ourselves: if I throw this weapon and it misses or if the opponent simply eats the strike and counters, am I in a worse position for it? We should strive to be economical not just in the delivery of our tools but also in our evaluation of potential risk/benefit too.

Another peril with the rear leg round kick is that its very power can cause grievous harm to the leg and foot that throws it. Several years ago a friend of mine who had a black belt in TKD was in a fight in which he thwacked his attacker with his patented round kick to the body. In his case it must be noted that his roundhouse kick was a considerable force of nature, often causing confusion locally among seismologists. "What was that? Another earthquake?? Call the press!" His master stroke was so punishing, so frightful that he succeeded in subduing two—yes two!—fighters with the same kick.

The problem was that he was one of them.

You see, sadly and somewhat predictably, his powerful and awe-inspiring kick was practiced in the dojo with pads on his feet to protect those surprisingly brittle foot bones. Against a live opponent, one armed with, well, elbows, the top of his foot quite literally exploded against his foe's elbow. He was fortunate that his opponent was too hobbled and intimidated to press his advantage afterwards because Captain Kicker was now Captain Ouch and couldn't walk.

It bears repeating: it's hard to break the bottom of your foot when throwing straight kicks (especially when you have shoes on). Straighter weapons offer more accuracy too so that we can limit (though, sadly, never completely eradicate) the danger of missing our target and hitting something we shouldn't.

Last with this point, a smart JKD fighter knows that even a modest groin kick is better than a massive round house kick that lands against sturdier stuff. This cuts both ways naturally and round house kicks can be countered with groin kicks easier than straighter blows.

SIDE KICK

One of the more amusing parts of Bruce Lee's self-defense volume in the Fighting Methods is the heavy reliance on the side kick to the knee. The kick itself isn't funny—it's devastating. What's hilarious is the brutal repetitiveness of it all. It would seem as though Lee was inclined to answer nearly every problem with the low side kick.

Attack from the side: side kick.

Attack while entering your car: side kick (poor Ted Wong).

Attack while leaning against a fence in an obviously bad neighborhood while wearing white-sissy pants: uh...side kick!

Yes, indeed, Bruce Lee's self-defense method certainly seems to have a way, now doesn't it? It's the method of SUPER SIDE KICK. One half suspects Bruce to don a cape and mask and show up bashing knee caps whenever there is crime at hand.

But seriously, such was his love for this simple and sweet tool. "It's like a boxer's jab, only it's much more damaging." I'll say!

If it can be said that the round kick is MT's signature, then the knee-wrecking side kick should be JKD's. It can be thrown so swiftly and with such devastating power that it can end any fight in a single moment. Its primary target—the knee and shin—are rather hard to defend and relatively easy to injure. With shoes/sneakers on the low side kick takes on all the more menacing a nature. Like the jab, it can be used differently as the tactical need arises. It can be thrown quickly to arrest an attack or even to set one up and, if the opponent is off-balance—perhaps pulling his weight back to avoid a punch—it can be thrown to break the leg. A straight leg is, after all, a broken leg!

For all of these reasons, it's easy to see why Lee gave it such a prominent place in his arsenal. As with all other tools in our toolbox it does have a few, though slight, imperfections. Chief amongst these is that it requires the hips to close off slightly, which leaves the kicker "turned around" just a bit if he's not careful. The straight kick keeps the hips facing forward and this allows a smoother transition to infighting than does the side kick, but constant, diligent practice can mute this potential drawback as the JKD fighter cleans up his delivery and recovery.

A good practice habit is to never try and kick too hard with the side kick but to cultivate a loose, snappy delivery. The power should come from the heavy leg snapping through the target, never by pushing. Aim with the heel or flat of the foot. Either will do nicely if you make contact squarely.

As noted previously, attacking a set opponent is forever frowned upon in a smart fighting method. Even an off-balance opponent can escape the wrath of the incoming shin/knee kick if it's telegraphed or thrown off line. Careful study and practice can help perfect the low kick into a veritable giant killer for any student. If a student never gets a chance to fire the side kick at the protected leg (preferably with baseball shin guards) of a mobile opponent, he'll never develop the fine sense of timing and accuracy needed to actually score. It is indeed a simple and powerful tool in our arsenal but, like the jab, simple doesn't mean easy.

The oblique kick is a type of cousin to the side kick, as JKD doesn't really use a rear leg side kick since doing so is quite uneconomical. Should the target present itself, though, and the lead leg be too close or have too much weight on it to quickly deliver a kick, the rear leg can spring into action. The oblique kick targets the opponent's vulnerable leg—preferably his shin and knee. Because of the angle it takes to the target and the closer range it's fired from it can often catch your foe seriously off balance and on the inside of the knee/shin, which can be utterly devastating.

CLOSE RANGE STRIKES

As previously mentioned, Jack Dempsey cautioned that the more you open your hook, which is to say the wider it becomes, the more you open your defense. Now hooks and uppercuts are particularly damaging tools used at close range, but the smart fighter must be disciplined with these short range beauties so as not to indulge in them from too far away. Should you launch a hook or uppercut from long-range you are leaving yourself quite rather at the mercy of your opponent's offensive inclinations since a great part of your body is now exposed. It's usually best to think of the bent-arm strikes as body blows as that will place you in the trenches where they belong and you'll be less likely to launch from the distance where you can get nailed by a punishing counter strike or grabbed and pulled into a grappling situation.

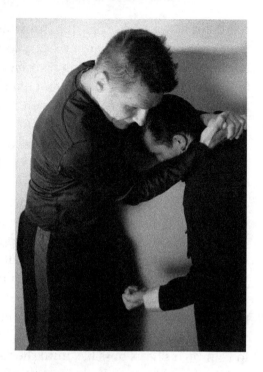

The long straight punches and kicks are JKD's forte, of course, but no amount of footwork and timing can guarantee that you won't end up in the trenches with an aggressive foe simply because the human body can go forward faster than it can go other directions. We should always be mentally prepared for the blitz attack. Ideally I'd like to hammer the over-aggressive foe with a straight lead or kick but such is the nature of fighting that sometimes that won't work. Sometimes he comes in firing so many swift blows of his own that I'm pinned down, caught flatfooted, and unable to keep the fight at a longer distance or safely establish contact-control/clinch.

On other occasions there is the possibility that we've stepped forward with our own strike and the opponent has grabbed us or covered up. Whatever the situation, hooks and uppercuts are the preferred strikes to deliver when we find ourselves in phone-booth warfare. The shortened range has robbed our straight punches of their supremacy and we must adjust accordingly.

In all-out bare knuckle fighting throwing hooks and uppercuts to the head is a dangerous game because it's easy to miss the chin and land higher on the head, possibly breaking your hand. Also, as we've already noted, for every inch of chin there's a foot of body. Should you find yourself in the trenches, perhaps nearly overrun by a frenzied assault, fire short, compact hooks and uppercuts at your enemy's torso, groin, and bladder. Range control is critical in fighting and especially in this instance. If your opponent grabs you behind the head and pulls you into a clinch, tee off on his bladder with the uppercuts. He won't like that much. MT fighters and grapplers far and wide get away with this particular tactic because it's illegal to bomb away at their village people. This is a prime example of an unnatural limitation on targeting giving fighters a false sense of security. The training of elbows and knees should be included in JKD but not at the expense of short hooks and uppercuts. Unless pinned down, the fist will always reach the target ahead of the elbow and punching in this manner allows for more rapidity than using the elbows. Practice these studiously on the heavy bag, head against the bag, elbows as close to your own side as possible, until they are loose, snappy, solid and fast. A determined low line body assault will assuredly make fighting in the trenches with you like trying to wrestle a Grizzly into the trunk of a car.

It's easy to forget that such blows—as short as they are—can have devastating effect. A bare-knuckle hook against the rib cage is a vicious thing. These in-close beauties are so effective in all-out fighting, in fact, that I think they should be worked as much as the straight lead and footwork. When combined with holding-and-hitting tactics they are absolutely lethal. Even the most well meaning JKD instructors who try and preserve the Wing Chun background of the method miss this oh-so sweet connection. A pak sao followed by a few compact hooks and uppercuts—maybe with a hook to the chin to finish the matter—is particularly effective in phone-booth warfare. In fact, I'd go so far as to say that this is the most neglected area of the boxing/Wing Chun connection since Wing Chun is a science of infighting and close-range hooks and uppercuts (which Wing Chun has too, by the way) work quite wonderfully at this range.

The mistake is that in boxing it's illegal to hold-and-hit. It's illegal because it works so well. But Wing Chun is a masterpiece of pushing, pulling and pinning—a more robust and scientific vertical grappling method really. Many Wing Chun students, on the other hand, have a bias against lowering their head while fighting so they don't think that such blows should be used in this context. But this prohibition is wrong-headed (sorry for the pun…I couldn't resist) because Wing Chun does not absolutely prohibit head movement. You see slight upper body angling in the Mook Jong form and at the end of Bui Jee. Pak and hit is never shown explicitly in any of the WC forms either but that doesn't mean there's a prohibition against it. What's more, a vigorous, scientific body attack is consistent with the lat-sau, jik chung (free hand, hit) principle of Wing Chun and often times saves us from seeking more complicated, less effective hand-chasing methods of in-fighting.

The issue should be that the JKD/WC fighter should only move as much as they need to —and to help facilitate a better position to strike or gain control of the opponent's balance/bridge. Many MT and MMA fighters are quite adept at gaining control of the neck and, despite our best efforts, we might still end up pulled forward. No worries, then. Why do something more complicated when a resounding attack to the body, bladder and groin are so easy?

Also, these wicked weapons of inside war are so terribly swift— coming in two's and three's and four's—that their dreadful power takes on all the more menace. Jack Dempsey is careful to remind us that there is a great difference between a hook and a swing. He says, "Many people mistake a swing for a hook because each blow travels in a circular direction. There's a life-and-death difference between the two blows, however. That difference originates in the hook's sharply bent elbow. In the swing, the arm is fully extended or nearly so."

We should always remember that in pure punching the fist is conveying force created by the body. True short range hooks and uppercuts are pure power punches—like the straights—in that they have the striking knuckles moving in the same direction of your bodyweight. This is something that swings cannot accomplish. Therefore a swing lacks a hook's explosiveness and safety. Dempsey says:

"Moreover, since it's almost impossible for the fist to land with its striking knuckles at the end of a hard swing, the landing usually is made with the palm-side knuckles or with the thumb knuckle or with the wrist. Any of those three landings is an invitation to a fracture. In addition, the swing is a doubly ineffective blow. It's easy for an opponent to block or to evade. And it lacks the explosiveness of the hook." Later he concludes, "Take the swing and toss it into the slop bucket and forget about it."

A variation of the hook and uppercut are something Dempsey called "shovel" hooks, thus named because of the hunching/shoveling motion used to deliver them. In the shovel hook, keep the arm and elbow as close to the body as possible, the fist angled up at 45 degrees, and slam your hip upward to shoot the fist into the target. The closer your arm is to your own body the better and safer for you. The power is coming from the legs and hips driving, whirling upward and the fist facing in the same direction at impact. The shovel is the closest range blow you can fire and requires mere inches of space.

A QUICK LOOK AT JEET KUNE DO & WING CHUN TRAINING

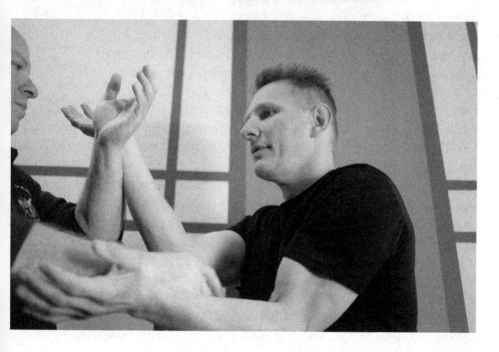

Wing Chun is not so much a fighting style as it is a very scientific system of structure and concepts. It is basically three empty hand forms—Sil Lim Tao, Chum Kui, and Bui Jee—a wooden dummy set, and two weapons forms. The bulk of traditional training in Wing Chun consists of these forms plus certain training drills, the most famous of which is Chi-Sao.

Students who hear me explain the origins of JKD (being Wing Chun-based) often ask, "why not just do Wing Chun entirely and skip the boxing/JKD training?" I think this is a rather logical question and one that is best answered in looking deeply at the core principles of Wing Chun, understanding their context, and in seeing JKD as a unique way of training and applying these principles. We must all admit that there are weaknesses built into everything that we do, and this is especially true of our fighting methods and the way we train them. The best we get is "prescriptions" in that we have a remedy for a particular problem but this remedy may and will introduce other issues too. The trick, for the doctor as well as the martial artist, is to logically manage these side-effects towards the goal of ultimate betterment.

Some JKD/WC stylists never spar, for example, claiming that there are drawbacks, instead of seeing sparring as a needed remedy to the the problem of getting realistic yet fairly safe "fight practice". Like a prescription, it has its drawbacks, but the alternative—never seeing real forceful punches coming your way—is probably worse than the prescription's side-effects.

Every Wing Chun student will start their training with the Sil Lim Tao form. This is rather odd for westerners who are more used to boxing and wrestling—I know it was for me. The weird little stance, the crossing of the hands in front of the body and the strange way of throwing the straight punch...it just didn't make much sense. Worse by far was the irritatingly slow fook-sao section. What the devil was that supposed to do for a man trying to learn how to fight? Seriously! Well, absent of the principles that this whole enterprise is trying to teach, I can't see why any student would stay with it and not run off to faster paced methods altogether.

But that's just it—SLT is teaching the students the very core of the art, the heart of the method right from day one. It's teaching the core theories of fighting the Wing Chun way and the structure through which the fighter will express those concepts. SLT is, as Tony Massengill points out in his book *Mastering Wing Chun*, "building the weapon." Chum Kui is the beginning of the Wing Chun fighter using that weapon—the structure and theory that he built in the first form. In the "bridge seeking form" he's learning how to find, or track, a moving target while he's in motion himself. Yes, the Wing Chun fighter is being given more theory—combat theory—as he moves that structure (the weapon) he's been building during the first form. The dummy form furthers this process by helping the student understand and correct the basic mistakes that tend to happen when their structure and theory engages in a fight. Mistakes will invariably be made and the fighter has in the mook jong a form that allows him to practice the habits of recovery so that they become instinctive.

All along this time the student is doing a variety of drills. Chi-sao is unarguably the chief of these but there is no disputing that sticking hands is not fighting; perhaps a bridge between the forms and fighting but that is all. Bui-jee is the emergency set of the method; it's the first aid kit. A Wing Chun fighter that utilizes the concepts of Bui-jee often is like a man going to the emergency room frequently—he needs to reconsider his lifestyle. Likewise, all the best fighting concepts and structure for the Wing Chun fighter are found in the first two forms and then tested on the dummy. Chi-sao helps the student learn many of these principles and put them in play reflexively while using "soft force"—which is to say, while relying on springy, relaxed muscles and skeletal structure.

You will notice that "fight practice" is omitted from this short survey. Most Wing Chun schools have their students punch the wall bag, do drills in a line, and so on; but for all this sound theory and scientific structure, Wing Chun training generally lacks what Bruce Lee called "aliveness" training. This is a sore spot, be sure, because you hear many clamor on about their deadly art working in the "real world" but yet you've never seen them train in a way where mistakes can happen. I will note here that if sticking hands practice is the "bridge" between forms and fighting, it is so because it tells the student that the other man will react and do things contrary to what you thought he'd do.

The great Wong Shun Leung, Wing Chun's Cus D'amato, fought often in "beimo" matches in order to test his theory and skills. These matches were rather critical for him in developing what we now know as WSLVT— or the Wong Shun Leung way. In testing the concepts and structure he was learning, Wong discovered certain things about the system and about himself. In doing so, he avoided Wing Chun's weakness and didn't stop learning only at the theoretical level. He put it to the test.

Now these matches did have certain rules. Only a fool would engage in combat to the death to test a theory. The trick is, again, in finding the correct balance between theory and practice. I think that Bruce Lee did this brilliantly in his development of JKD. He didn't reinvent the wheel; boxing always had means testing procedures (sparring) and preparation drills (bag work, mitt training) that further bridged the gap between forms and fighting. Again, only a fool and/or a criminal keeps getting into fights, whereas the smart and serious student endeavors to work his game as scientifically and as safely as possible, towards the end goal of having reflexive self-defense skills that he can count on and that he knows work for him.

There is simply no perfect way to do this. All approaches are fraught with some danger and certain drawbacks. That is what Lee was talking about with his more confusing statements about having "no way as way" and so on. JKD is very much a style of training the Wing Chun concepts and structure and it incorporates much boxing—not willy-nilly—but only those parts of it that compliment Wing Chun's own core principles and assist in the application and testing thereof. Just as Wong Shun Leung went out and battled the other styles that populated the Hong Kong kung-fu scene of his day, at our school we cross train frequently against boxers and MMA fighters. Wong commented once that he preferred working against boxers exactly because they were quite formidable and could punch with power from either hand at any time. JKD takes this advice and does the same.

Clearly, the JKD/WC fighter is at a disadvantage sparring against such stylists but that isn't the point. At our Academy we have both boxing and MMA programs so it's rather easy to cross-train, but in any event, most of these individuals are more than happy to "work" with people who'd like to get some experience against them and their styles—they're curious too. The issue is going in to train against an extremely well-conditioned athlete who will move and hit. My thoughts were always that if I could go in there with good fighter/athletes and do okay, then I'd be that much more able to handle the average knucklehead on the street who wasn't so well trained. I'll get more into the best forms of such training/sparring in another volume and, more appropriately, in videos, but suffice it to say that all of the theory and structure we develop absolutely must be applied somehow. JKD's attitude should be one of smart training and preparation in order to apply the principles learned in Wing Chun. And, like I've said before, this isn't the only way to do it but it must get done. If a fighter doesn't have live experience with people throwing hard shots at them, they are an accident waiting to happen. And if a student doesn't get enough time in working on actually hitting moving targets, he's quite limited his opportunities for success in a real encounter against an opponent that will be moving—and firing back.

The previous material in the book—the techniques—have been around for thousands of years. Boxers of old used low kicks at times, in fact. What JKD has done, using Wing Chun as its pivot point, is make the delivery and training of these tools more systematic. And, in light of this, JKD offers a unique training environment for those that are so inclined. No measure of seeking personal improvement should be left out for the student, which is why Lee—like his mentor Wong Shun Leung—was always tinkering around against the other styles and so on. The object isn't to turn your JKD into boxing or MMA or Muay Thai but to get a chance to train in a dynamic environment against well-prepared opposition and see for yourself what you can and can't do. Real fighters won't just stand there and let you hit them with eye-jabs and groin kicks, after all. Muay Thai fighters, for instance, are well aware of their weaknesses. A MT instructor once told me that he knew his groin was exposed but, he said, most other fighters aren't truly trained to land such a blow whereas he was trained to score his own so the point was moot. That's the whole point of Bruce's approach. He got out there to make sure he could do what he thought he could. If, he reasoned, he couldn't land a stiff jab in a controlled sparring session, he knew he had no hope of doing something more complex.

Also, the JKD student, following the sterling lead of the founder, seeks to be in the very best condition they can be in. That some resistance to this remains today within JKD/WC circles astonishes me greatly. Why would you not want to be in the greatest physical condition possible? Isn't martial arts about self-improvement? Some contend that when they use their skills "properly" the fight won't last but a few seconds anyway so it doesn't matter that they're in such desultory condition that they couldn't run around the block. Good luck surviving the coming zombie apocalypse—we'll all need cardio!

But, seriously, what kind of talk is this? It sounds eerily close to the bluster of men before every war that goes on longer and kills far more than anyone dared to fathom. The South did it in the Civil War; Europe did it before the Great War; Hitler again when he attacked Stalin; Bush with his ill-planned "shock-and-awe." When you plan for your enemy to fall easily, you're setting yourself up for disaster. And, for goodness sake, what man would go into a gun fight with only one bullet?

In the movie *Crocodile Dundee* there is that classic scene where a mugger pulls a knife on Mick and demands his wallet. Mick is strangely unconcerned that someone is threatening his life with an edged weapon though. His female companion, bewildered by his odd amusement and calm, pleads with him to comply with the criminal's demand. "He's got a knife," she implores him. Then Dundee utters that famous line, "that's not a knife." The mugger runs off in terror as Dundee pulls out a near machete masquerading as a knife—easily dwarfing his own weapon.

This is how the JKD student looks at physical conditioning. Running, lifting weights, diet, stretching, training—these are all means to improving our physical performance so that we might personally be that machete against a switch-blade. Your body is the weapon, after all, and Lee was fond of reminding students that far too little time was spent on developing the person engaging in the combat compared to the techniques used by the person. If we can improve our endurance, speed, strength and flexibility it will only help to serve us as fighters. What's more, other attributes like timing, distance control and accuracy can be developed and fine-tuned through consistent, smart sparring and sparring drills. JKD is a science of martial training, leaving as little to chance as safely possible.

Whether we look at the NFL, NBA, or MLB, athletes are bigger, stronger, faster and better prepared than previous generations. Bruce Lee helped pave a way for that in martial arts too and we do well to approach our personal development—our attribute training—just like he did.

SIL LIM TAO

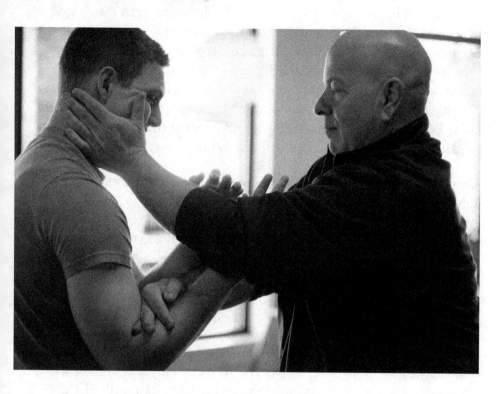

We now turn our attention to Wing Chun's breathtakingly simple foundation—that splendid "little idea"—Sil Lim Tao. We won't cover the whole of the form in this book, as I believe that such should be covered in another volume entirely, but it must be addressed as it is, quite simply, the cornerstone of both Wing Chun and its derivative, Jeet Kune Do.

At my school we begin teaching SLT from the first day in our JKD classes while also doing plenty of reps of the previously detailed striking. It's important to tell the students that what they are seeing in SLT is not just one "little" or "young" idea but really a series of concepts, structural underpinnings, and technique introductions. The movements of the form are connected sequentially but not necessarily conceptually. Each part does not flow necessarily to the next no more than B has to follow A in conversation. It is unfortunately true that many misguided WC students try to fight and spar like they are doing one of the Wing Chun forms but this isn't WC's fault as much as it is the fault of the instructor not giving the student the proper guidance.

A real WC instructor approaches SLT like a good guitar instructor would approach his instrument. A student absolutely has to learn the chords, which is to say that they have to know the "structure" of the instrument in expressing music. Still, though, the goal is to make music, not play chords. Music is the goal and the chords are the means to that end. SLT is like the guitarist learning his chords and scales; he isn't going to play like that but he will play (express himself) through them. It is true that many WC students--intoxicated by the coolness of the system—don't fully understand this and lose the forest to the many techniques.

Many JKDers fault WC because they see clueless WC students sparring/fighting, but that's like giving up on music because you've heard one too many bad garage bands. Instead, we should look at Wing Chun like we look at boxing—we think of its champions, not its no-hopers. In Wing Chun, watch Tony Massengill, Gary Lam, David Peterson, etc. Watch how these men use their SLT-based structure creatively to solve fistic problems. True Wing Chun masters have not been enslaved to their system, they've made it their slave.

We should be well aware that trying to master JKD without Sil Lim Tao is like having a job that doesn't pay you. You can only stay at it for so long before you need to go do something else. Gary Lam calls SLT the foundation fortress of Wing Chun and so it is. If a JKD student doesn't have this as part of his/her training—not just the movements but the heart and soul of the concepts too—then they will invariably need to seek out another system to complete their JKD. Old-school boxing is not a complete art like Wing Chun, and the regrettable intellectual wanderings of JKD over the past few decades have largely been because the ideas expressed in this form have not been understood and practiced.

For our purposes, let us look at the first part of SLT and see what it's teaching us.

The form starts, of course, with the weird little stance—toes facing in. It should be pointed out to the JKD student immediately that this isn't a stance that he'll fight out of. The purpose of the Yee Jee Kim Yung Ma is to instill in the student the proper structure through which to fight from. Remember: Wing Chun is primarily a close-range fighting system with it's footwork and base more rooted than boxing because if I'm "up on my toes" in close, my opponent can easily knock me about. Free movement phase—or long range footwork is different than close range footwork. At long range we are most concerned with speed and mobility whereas once contact has been made base and stability become far more important. We see this in MMA today when a striker moves into a clinch he changes his stance slightly to account for the reality of close-quarter combat/grappling.

The stance is training us to move with structure and draw power from the floor as well as conditioning our legs for the rigorous demands of fighting.

Next, we see the arms crossing in front of the body, first low and then high. This is not to imply some kind of blocking procedure but, rather, it's informing us of the all-important center-line. We want to attack and defend the center for the very reason that the body's most vulnerable targets—eyes, nose, throat—are on or close to center of mass. People just don't make a habit of blocking punches with their nose or throat. The form is telling us right from the start that our goal is to take the center and preserve our own.

Also, right along with center-line, there is the concept of chui-ying/by-ying, which is the important corollary of center-line—facing. When we engage our opponent we don't want to be "turned-over" with one side too extended. Doing so allows the opponent the option of counter attack by grabbing/wrestling as we're in no position to fend off such tactics. This is a major weakness in my beloved Ted Wong's approach to JKD. He was certainly right that the extreme turning of the shoulder gives the straight lead more reach—and this option is certainly still on the table should the situation allow it—but it leaves us, for all intents and purposes, one-handed, and that is no way to fight an aggressive opponent. I will add that old adage—styles make fights. If you are faster than your foe and want to keep whacking him silly at long range with the lead hand and foot, that's great. But if that's all you are trained to do and your opponent wants to charge in, you're going to need this structure or you'll be run over.

The very next thing we do in SLT is throw the straight punch. Wing Chun is not about all the fancy hand techniques—it's about punching the bad guy in the nose and/or hitting him in the center hard, fast, and often. If he opens his center up we should be hitting him. If we keep the facing concept and apply it with the straight punch, we will have maximum opportunity to throw an overwhelming attack in that we'll have both hands in play. The boxing concept uses too much shoulder rotation on its punches and that allows the enemy too much time in which to counter and/or grab. In this, Wing Chun is a terrific anti-grappling system because it's structure discourages grabs by keeping both limbs in play and, importantly, in front of the trunk.

Once we lose facing we are in grave danger of being overwhelmed by a charge. Notice how grapplers and Muay Thai fighters are always squared on the inside. To do otherwise is quite dangerous. Thus, the combined concepts of center-line, facing, and straight hitting with both sides gives the Wing Chun fighter a significant advantage not seen in other systems. Note that in the *Bruce Lee's Fighting Method* series we see Lee using the chain punch from exactly this set and it informs us that both the long and short straight punch are used interchangeably in JKD.

By-ying is basically the idea that since we're at our offensive best when facing our foe with shoulders squared, we endeavor not to let our foe do the same to us. If he throws a straight punch or push we can use pak sao, for example, along with a straight hit to eradicate his facing position. The goal is to place the enemy where his shoulders aren't facing me while mine are facing him. Doing so will give me a rather significant, violent advantage in a fight—one that when combined with the rapid striking this position affords, as well as pushing forward, should end matters quite satisfactorily for me.

Next we do the very slow and repetitive fook-sao section of SLT. There is much to be said about this important section, but suffice it to say that it is building on the previous concepts and teaching us to "chase" the enemy's center—to hit him—and not baby-sit his hands. Sometimes this is over-simplified. To just try and hit the guy without reference to chui-ying/by-ying, center control, and the elbow position of fook-sao will likely mean that we end up trading with the enemy and this is the last thing we want to do. The fook-sao concept in this part of the form is preparing us to engage, subdue (control), and attack at the same time through proper structure. During close-range fighting I cannot use the fook-sao concept if I'm not facing, so these concepts must all be integrated, which is exactly why they're in a form in the first place. The rest of the Wing Chun system is basically an extrapolation of these core principles. The rest of the forms and training drills are, when properly considered, ways of applying these concepts and/or overcoming obstacles to their application.

All errors in Wing Chun can generally be attributed to the misunderstanding of or failure to apply these core principles.

For example, there has been controversy in JKD circles over the application of trapping. Many critics point out that you can't trap people in a real fight. Trapping defenders—all standing about like Lee vs. Bob Wall in *Enter the Dragon*—insist that it can and the dissenters just haven't practiced enough. Who's right? Well...the critics are right. Trapping doesn't work the way JKD has traditionally understood it.

Now, hang on...take a breath (if you're an Original JKD student that swears that sound trapping skills are the answer to the world's problems) and consider what's really happening. In Wing Chun there is really no talk about trapping—at least not trapping an opponent who is fighting in a fixed position. Cross-arm drills like pak-da, etc., are merely drills to work on mechanics and basically discarded once the student reaches advanced chi-sao level where they can work close-range against a "live" opponent. The JKD student who has never fully understood SLT concepts and seen the rest of Wing Chun will not understand that trapping drills are just

that—drills. Drills are a means to an end and we should be on-guard lest we fail to see the finger pointing away at something more important (such as the concept of "bridging" which comes in the second form). Of course, I know that some devoted "trappers" out there in JKD-land are now wanting to give me the finger, but stay with me a little longer please.

Imagine for a moment that you've never seen a boxing match and you have no idea what boxing is supposed to look like. In this uneducated state you happen to wander in to a boxing gym and observe a boxer training. We can only imagine what odd conclusions you might draw when you witness the fighter hitting the speed bag. "Well, that's insane," you'd declare, puzzling over the odd spectacle. Next, witness the heavy bag work. "Why

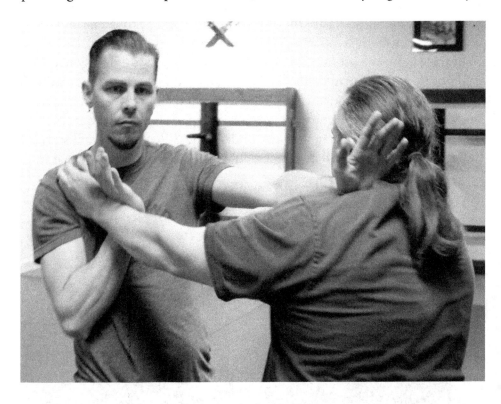

do you think that you're going to fight some dude hanging from a chain? That's madness!" And how is skipping rope going to help in a fight?

Now, obviously, knowing what boxing is, you aren't puzzled by these unique training practices because you know where they're headed. The problem with JKD students often times is that they've never seen the rest of Wing Chun or—just as importantly—properly understood the core concepts of the system. Wing Chun's SLT is a collection of core principles and techniques; it is not a fight simulator but, rather, as Tony Massengill superbly puts it, SLT is a process of "building the weapon".

But back to the vexing trapping issue for the moment. What's caused the most trouble is that JKD is often guilty of confusing the training drill for what the drill is intended to prepare the trainee for. It goes by many names in Wing Chun circles: bridging, crossing hands, linking. In boxing and MMA, it's often referred to as clinching. Whatever the name—it's the science of infighting, and trapping drills like the more advanced drills of lop-sao and chi-sao, which are means to an end--safe and progressive ways of preparing us to engage in close range combat. This is to say that if you're practicing, and going from one compound trap to the next against a partner who doubles as a somewhat life-like mook-jong, you need a new approach. Sadly, you're like a boxer who hits the bag but never spars (although in fairness, bag work is far superior than these dead trapping drills in developing fighting skills because you'll often see better footwork in morgues than in "trapping" classes).

Trapping as a tactic is all fine and dandy, but I can't imagine a boxer getting into an argument over hooking or crossing or some such thing. As it goes, since they're out there sparring and training against live partners who are moving and shooting back blows of their own, boxers don't run into such compartmental nonsense as this.

A student who properly understands the core principles of Wing Chun as explained and practiced in SLT will no doubt wonder why he's spending time trapping when he could be shifting to achieve a superior angle. No, trapping doesn't work in real fights if it means that we're chasing hands rather than chasing/facing center and the bad guy can't get squared to us because of our pivoting and footwork. Sticking to and applying the core principles gives the Wing Chun fighter a decided advantage in the trenches and no matter how good your long game is, fights often go to close range. The aforementioned and much to be praised Jim Driscoll admits in his book that a good boxer must still clinch and that such is a staple of sound defense—and footwork! Should we have a robust understanding of the whole Wing Chun system we'll see that it's a highly advanced clinching range art that is very unique to the world of martial arts.

Regardless of all the praise we've heaped upon old-school boxing in this volume—greatly deserved—boxing has its obvious limitations—not least of which is its clinch game—and we should see it as the proverbial boat to get us across the water. Should we complete the Wing Chun system, though, we will have a far more advanced methodology than boxing--one that handles close range fighting with significantly greater science than boxing. The object of Wing Chun, though, is to have no way as way; it is aware of its own limitations and is, therefore, a system of moving concepts. I have tried my best to illustrate the unknown by the known in using boxing comparisons to Wing Chun which is to say that Ali's boxing was different than Dempsey's boxing.

Wing Chun, being a conceptual system, offers, like boxing, a broad range of interpretive and application opinions. But to get to this point Wing Chun wisely gives us three empty hand forms—plus the wooden dummy set—to guide us through its major combat theories. Restraint and simplicity are the key. We could have had hundreds of forms passed down but we have only these precisely because people are prone—as we've already discussed—to complicate matters hopelessly.

I joke in my school that SLT is the perfect American form because it's all about you. The major point of the form is to develop the proper structure by practice of the stance (yee jee kim yueng ma) as it relates to each arm/hand movement. Consistent practice will give the student an intuitive feel for appropriate technique by drilling into them the use of the center-line and elbow moving line. Once the student has done the form to the point that the body "feels" immediately where the proper structure is, they can move onto drills like Chi-Sao and the second form where shifting and stepping are practiced. This distinction is critical. SLT provides the optimal facing position for a WC fighter and prepares them for the generation of great force through waist energy (yui ma), stepping (toh ma), last second energy and two way energy. All of this is best achieved when SLT has been mastered.

Furthermore, SLT introduces the major "saos" of the Wing Chun system or, if you will, the "seed" hands of fook, tan, and bong. By practicing how these hand techniques properly align with the stance the student not only learns how to use a pak-sao or a palm strike/push, they learn to use these techniques with optimal body structure rather than just muscular force. In JKD class when we practice holding and hitting the students have the proper reference for a pak-sao, a lan-sao, etc., because of the form. In fact, all of our fighting techniques are right here in the first form. It's much like learning your ABC's; we're always using the alphabet when we communicate and we're always using Sil Lim Tao when we're fighting. If you were to go back and compare the striking techniques we've already covered in this book you'll notice that all of them are derivatives of SLT directly or its ideas—even it's kicking. All we're doing, frankly, is practicing the punching and kicking concepts of Wing Chun.

So, in practicing SLT we're developing proper structure, the basic techniques, and finally we're being introduced to some of the core WC fighting concepts. Again, the concept of facing is critical in WC theory. This doesn't imply, however, that the WC fighter is to advance helter-skelter at an opponent when he is facing too! Think about it: if I'm at my offensive best when I have a facing position (therefore I'm able to use any/all of my limbs in attack and defense equally) then, DUH!, so is my rival. A smart instructor will point this out to the student so that he doesn't end up over-simplifying Wing Chun, which is to say leave out very relevant details. A student that hasn't been properly taught in this area will often attack recklessly, without any concern for what position the enemy is in. Wing Chun is about control. We want to intercept what comes, follow what's retreating and attack where there's emptiness. If our enemy is in a strong position we should not attack but when we do we should use proper structure and facing.

To the JKD student so inclined, a careful study of SLT under the right instructor will yield surprising results. Take, for example, this whole notion of stop-hitting... it's in the very first part of the form as is straight hitting. And when we practice the fook sao we are really learning the concepts—physically as well as tactically as there can be no real division in fighting—of simultaneous attack and defense through structure

and position, and the principle of hitting where there's emptiness (lat sau jik chung). These were not, after all, just brilliant ideas of Bruce Lee but tried and true principles of the WC he'd learned from Ip Man. Plus, the practice of the fook sao part of the form gives us the idea of doing two things at once—it's the idea where trapping comes from, in fact; you're subduing the foe's attack with one of your own.

Now, again, it hasn't been my intent to offer you a full breakdown of SLT in this volume, but to put it—and Wing Chun's central role in JKD—in proper perspective. As I've said previously, it isn't my belief that this is the only way to teach Jeet Kune Do—using old-school boxing and Wing Chun—but I do think it's the most logical. There have been some mighty controversies throughout the years in regard to who was certified to teach JKD which is quite ironic considering what we're talking about. Bruce Lee had two years of Wing Chun under Ip Man and was in no way able or qualified to teach. And by everyone's admittance, those he trained he used as much as guinea pigs as anything else.

To say, therefore, that Bruce Lee certified someone is somewhat of a dubious thing. What did he certify the person in exactly? What

was the body of work? Wing Chun? He couldn't have...impossible. Boxing? Lee never boxed past his teenage years and who, for crying out

loud, gets certified in boxing? Oh...perhaps it was his modified Wing Chun. But think, dear reader—who can teach a modified something that they've barely learned themselves without causing quite a bit of perplexity and uncertainty? And, indeed, isn't this exactly what's happened? Or perhaps you say he did pass on this thing we've been talking about called Jeet Kune Do. But again, we are back in the same distress, for JKD has to be exactly what I've been saying it is and not something esoteric, and nebulous for the reasons put forth.

We are not to conclude from this that Lee himself was some miscreant hell-bent on leading the gullible masses astray. Absolutely not, dear reader! His aforementioned shortcomings and imperfections were not the result of nefariousness but of the natural limitations that beset him due to his moving to America and being unable to finish his Wing Chun training. To my knowledge he was never anything but honest about his background in regard to his training even though students in America would have had little chance of finding out the lie had he indulged in one. To his credit, he was honest and honorable to a great degree.

More still, the laudable Mr. Lee was a tireless worker and dreamer. His status as an icon is richly deserved in many ways because his character is the well from which his fame was drawn. People all over the world are drawn to him, inspired by him, and rightly admire him. My statements of these aforementioned facts are not to diminish him but rather to save his beloved martial art from the very people who have blindly exalted him to the point where they've lost sight of reality. If we are to think of JKD as the personal vehicle of Bruce Lee only—his own unique expression (again: of what??) then what is there to practice? If JKD is just a concept never to be fully defined by those in the know—a wonderfully gnostic way of perpetuating the irrational claims of a privileged few—there truly is no use in training in this thing at all. The years are passing; as always time has its way and is the greatest, most unrelenting of all foes. Already the younger students have barely any experience with Mr. Lee at all. They know Jet Li and Jackie Chan perhaps—*Kung Fu Panda* even—but there's no true emotional connection to Lee.

So, if JKD is to continue it cannot be solely on Lee's legacy but upon the basis of these methods I've outlined. We court obsolescence if JKD is taught and marketed as Bruce Lee rather than the two methods embraced by Lee. Boxing and Wing Chun have outlived him despite his railings against the restrictions of styles and methods. In truth, the question should never have been man versus method. It should have been and still should be: is the method an accurate representation of the truth? Those in the Lee camp that believe in him almost as the little-Deity rather than the little-Dragon fail to see him as just a man trying to see the truth for what it was through the methods he'd been taught.

When we offer JKD students a Wing Chun-based JKD and teach the true principles of the Ip Man system, we actually give them the tools of liberation about which Lee spoke so passionately, and with which he moved so many hearts. This, I believe, is the true JKD heritage and the only one that can prevent Lee's valid interpretations of Wing Chun and boxing from disappearing altogether in the coming generations, or in the least, being relegated to the shadows. Wing Chun and boxing live on because they are methods that accurately, correctly correspond to the reality they address. A Bruce Lee-based JKD rather than a Wing Chun/boxing JKD is like an old band going on tour again, trying to recapture the old glory but gaining no new fans and reminding its old ones that they are, well, old.

Personally, those things that I have loved so immeasurably about Lee—his emphasis on simplicity and honesty being chief among them—are embodied in the Wing Chun system and that is where the seed was first planted in his mind and heart. For a man that just wants to learn to fight pretty well quickly, let him take up the combat sports for they will serve him well but they will not make of him a martial artist. Wing Chun, with Sil Lim Tao leading the way, has already enriched thousands of lives by not only making warriors but even philosophers through the correct balance of practice and theory. That some Wing Chun students fight poorly and misapply the lessons of the method is no knock against it no more than a bad writer cancels out Shakespeare. All of the things—all of the lofty concepts that flowed from Lee's lips and pen—they are within the Wing Chun system and he was their student and JKD is its creative offspring.

Sifu Aaron Bouchillon

Sifu Mark Strickland
As cool as the other side of the pillow.

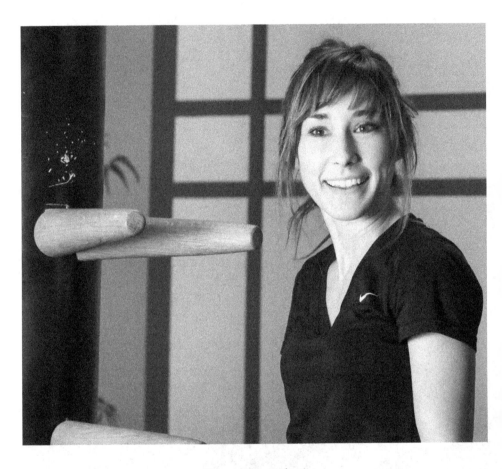

Kacy Hatmaker
JKD Assistant Instructor

Jesse Moshure
JKD & Wing Chun Instructor

Jazilyn Wiley
Junior Black Belt and kid's assistant instructor

Caleb Savage

Jeff Hatmaker
JKD, Wing Chun, Boxing student and all-around good guy

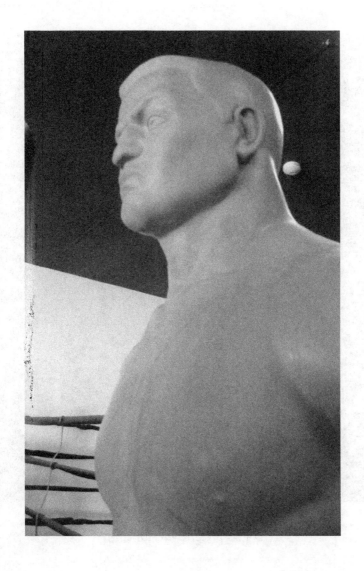

Bob
A man who never complains

My Sifu, Master Tony Massengill
www.efficientwarrior.com

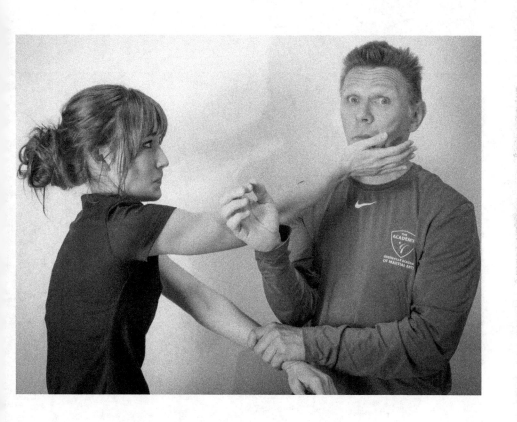

Sifu Aaron before he's had his coffee.

Sifu Aaron after he's had his coffee.

CPSIA information can be obtained
at www.ICGtesting.com
Printed in the USA
BVHW072146010120
568341BV00018B/1519/P